HIRING'S
SECRET SAUCE

What recruitment agencies know about hiring that you don't
...Until now!

Gary Costa

Content Warning:
Only open if you want to outperform your competitors.
* Does not contain any stats, graphs, or big data.

"I'm convinced that nothing we do is more important than hiring and developing people. At the end of the day you bet on people, not on strategies."

Lawrence Bossidy, Author, and CEO (retired)
AlliedSignal Corporation (later Honeywell Corporation)

"Some people can do one thing magnificently, like Michelangelo, and others make things like semiconductors or build 747 airplanes — that type of work requires legions of people. In order to do things well, that can't be done by one person, you must find extraordinary people."

Steve Jobs, co-founder of Apple Inc.

"Hiring people is an art, not a science, and resumes can't tell you whether someone will fit into a company's culture."

Howard Schultz, Chairman Emeritus at Starbucks

Table of Contents

Preface

This book has a singular purpose: to give you the method and the tools to hire the top 10% of employees - so that your business can establish an advantage over its competitors.

That's exactly what I've done for over twenty years – identify and hire the top 10% of performers. It's the only reason employers have paid the fees I charge. I help them establish and maintain, a competitive advantage through the people they hire.

I've taken my most effective techniques, and combined them with the tools my recruitment agency uses on every single hiring exercise. These are true professional agency tools – the exact same ones.

I've placed those tools on my website. Together with this book, they make up Hiring's Secret Sauce. You can visit our website using this QR code:

Hiring can be thought of as a skill or a trade (much like carpentry). Ordinarily it takes a few years to become a good carpenter, but that's mostly because you need to master a physical skill set (sawing, hammering, chiseling etc.). With hiring, you just need the right tools and a proven system that works. Hiring's Secret Sauce gives that to you. Anyone in business can do this – and I do mean anyone. Your company's bottom line and the performance of all your staff will be improved as a result. Oh yes, I forgot. Its other purpose is to give you a bit of a laugh. Feel free to drop me a line and let me know if I succeeded in that.

How to use this book

Each of the fourteen chapters in this book follows the main steps of the hiring process, and interspersed through those chapters are the real secrets to hiring - written up as fourteen (14) separate ingredients. Reading this book from the beginning will ensure you pick up all the ingredients of the Secret Sauce. Once you've done that, use the book as a refresher by jumping back into any Chapter such as Interviewing, Reference Checking, etc.

For those reading this in paperback form, there's a blank page at the end to handwrite all the ingredients you pick up through the book – it then becomes a handy summary page. If you're on an E-reader, I recommend writing the ingredients down in a file and keeping it with you whenever you start a new hiring exercise and certainly, whenever you are dealing with candidates. Simply re-reading those ingredients should provide most of the reminding you will need on what to do for that given step.

What this book doesn't include

I have deliberately avoided the use of statistics, graphs, or big data. Instead, I've used real-life experiences. I'm a believer in the learnings available through personal interactions.

These human interactions can inform us for both what to do, and what not to do. I have learnt that people "are who they are" – that you cannot significantly change them and in fact, you shouldn't try because you can rely on this when hiring. In truth, the Secret Sauce is largely based on this fact – that once you truly understand a person-candidate, you will then know whether they are right for your job vacancy (or not).

While we don't use big data or stats, we do touch upon the social sciences (Organizational Psychology). It has been used in the creation of our proformas – most notably our interview proforma. We also discuss psychometric assessments (also known as personality profiles). They are a valuable tool, and their correct use is discussed in Chapter 12.

A final word...

About the 10% of people, 20% of people, 70% of people quote on the back cover. It's something that has never sat comfortably with me. The quote was first attributed to a speech given by the President of Columbia University (New York) in 1931. Since that time, people have debated the percentages in each of the three categories, while others have argued that it's simply not true.

When it comes to this book, the more relevant question is this: Assuming there's some truth to the quote, is it caused by nature or nurture?

Personally, I first heard this quote from one of my clients. They certainly believed it, and I helped them hire the 10%.

As you move through this book, you're going to notice a lot of the focus is on excluding candidates as you progress toward finding "The One". You're also going to notice a skeptical or doubting overtone in a lot of the chapters. That's because for over twenty years, my experience has been that many candidates just want to present as more capable, more accomplished, and just plain old better, than they actually are. Is it just the job application environment that makes them act that way? I'm not sure but once again, I wish it wasn't so. Rest assured, Hiring's Secret Sauce has it covered.

TALES FROM THE V🔒ULT

The candidate who fell to earth (with apologies to David Bowie).

Things are looking good with this candidate. I'm hiring an analyst for a finance company and, as I've done this many times before, I know when I've found the right type of candidate. Right now, there's just one question left to ask.

It's known as a situational-behavioral question. I've added it as a custom question to my Interview proforma because it's extremely important to this employer (my client) - let's call them ABC Financial.

Robert, imagine you're attending a company meeting, and you've been asked to outline your strategy for a new client of ABC Financial. After your presentation (and after hearing the strategies of your other colleagues), a decision is made to adopt one of your colleagues' strategies instead of yours. What do you do now?

Robert answers that he would ask for the opportunity to present his calculations and formulas to the group one more time, to prove his strategy is the best one for the client.

"Ultimately, I'll accept the decision, but next time I'll do even better so you just can't argue against it. Next time, I'll prove my strategy is superior". This answer ruled Robert out of contention. I had worked with ABC Financial to create the job description for this role, and this one custom question summarized the collegial style of the company – the way they worked together to get the very best outcome for their clients. Robert didn't work that way. This single (seriously wrong) answer highlights why our Chapter 1 topic is such an important part of the Secret Sauce.

There is, however, an endnote to Robert's story...

You see, on a personal level, I quite liked Robert. He was polite, respectful, had achieved good academic results, and brought an obvious passion for the finance industry, and passion is something I rate highly in candidates.

I believed he could make a worthwhile contribution to my client – right up until he gave that seriously wrong answer.

Perhaps above all, was his gracious acceptance of my rejection at the end of our interview. He appeared genuinely grateful for having been given the opportunity. "A young graduate with some promise" is what I thought to myself. I was hopeful for Robert that he would learn from the experience and secure a similar opportunity elsewhere. Of course, in the back of my mind was the question: "Could he change"?

While writing this book, I decided to check on Robert's journey since our interview some years ago.

What I found was that he has worked for several different employers during the last five years – his career is too mobile. I might be able to attribute a couple of those short tenures to less-than-ideal employers, but it's unlikely it was the factor in each move he made.

I suspect that what the Secret Sauce method uncovered about Robert's work style (which is a function of his personality), has presented issues for him wherever he's gone.

Most of the time, the Secret Sauce method works by identifying the right candidate for you.

At other times, it saves you from hiring the wrong candidate.

Both are just as important as each other.

Chapter 1

Castles made of sand
fall into the sea eventually

(Job descriptions... with apologies to Jimi Hendrix)

You wouldn't risk it, would you?

Chapter rating

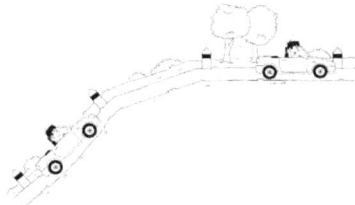

A little bit of hard going, then easy.

I'm going to get the unexciting stuff out of the way now, so we can move on to the more entertaining stories, – but this first chapter does come with a **BIG** statement:

If I said to you that there was one thing you could do – just *one* thing that would ensure you get your hiring right 80% of the time, you'd take it wouldn't you?

Of course you would.

But here's the thing…

If I were a betting man, I would lay $100 down right now that you won't take up the central piece of advice offered here in Chapter 1. I know that's a bold (and somewhat harsh) thing to say.

I'm making this call because doing what this chapter recommends, is like being told to clean up your bedroom when you're a teenager. You've heard the message, but you're not going to do what you're told because:

a. the message came from your parents and,

b. you never listen to your parents.

Now, roughly as many of you who *did* clean up your bedrooms when your parents asked you to, is about how many of you will take up this Chapter 1 recommendation.

So, are you the kind of person that did (and will) do those kinds of activities that are boring – and maybe even slightly difficult, because you are disciplined and conscientious enough to know you really should (and that doing so *will* benefit you) or, are you the kind of person that will just deal with the inevitable mess (which we know only gets worse the longer we leave it) because, well, – because there are more interesting and fun things to do out there?

Now, if you're in that second group (and that's perfectly fine), I'm going to suggest that if you want to, just jump straight ahead to Chapter 2 or Chapter 3 where the fun stories begin to ramp up - or just jump ahead to any chapter that grabs your interest. If you like what you read there, then come back here later.

You can probably guess what I'm up to – I want to get you to embrace all the key messages (all the ingredients) in this book. I'm hoping you like (and believe) what you read in the more entertaining chapters, and that the enjoyment you receive there tells you that perhaps there's something worthwhile to learn here in Chapter 1 – and you come back.

Really, I don't mind. Just go wherever you want to. It's your book. You can do whatever you like ☺

And...

There's another reason behind this Chapter 1 challenge. It's a subtle introduction to a central theme that runs through this book. It unfolds as we begin to explore how personality drives the actions of the staff you're looking to hire. You'll see what I mean...

The base of the secret sauce

Most sauces have a base ingredient that really establishes their flavor. If there's one ingredient in the Hiring Secret Sauce that is most like the "base" ingredient, then it would be this – the Job Description (hereafter referred to as the J.D).

The one thing that has proven itself *time and again* over the last twenty years, is that by building a good J.D and consistently referring to it throughout the hiring exercise (and refusing to deviate from it), I get the right result every time. When I (or more usually the employer) accepted a candidate whose qualifications, competencies or preferences did not match the J.D, then the hiring exercise either failed, or the glue didn't hold[1] (meaning the new employee left or failed within a short period of time).

1. In Appendix 2, I've listed the handful of reasons why the glue "holds", and you enjoy hiring success, along with the many reasons why hiring exercises fail (and I explain how to recognise and avoid those scenarios).

Adhering to the Job Description will enable you to get the right result 80% of the time. I use the term *result* because in some cases, the Job Description informs you that you are presently Interviewing, Testing, Reference Checking or Making an offer, to the *wrong* candidate. It prevents a mismatch, as often as it confirms the right person.

To raise your success rate above 80% you just add the other ingredients contained in this book. To be realistic, it isn't possible to get it right 100% of the time because we're dealing with people not numbers, and there are just too many uncontrollable factors involved. However, you can certainly aim for a 90% or higher success rate[2]. Let me show you how...

Once you've absorbed the secret sauce in this book, you'll realise that hiring is a lot like riding a bicycle. Once learnt, you can always do it. You might be a little rusty after a long break, but you'll soon get back into the rhythm.

---

2. *Success at my recruitment agency is defined as the placed candidate remaining employed for a minimum of 12 months. Using that metric, my success rate over the past 20 years is 96%. Some have remained employed for 10 years or more, with many going on to achieve promotions. They were all hired using the techniques outlined in this book, along with the Secret Sauce proforma documents available on our website*

And conveniently, it just happens that a bicycle wheel is the perfect way to illustrate the different parts of the hiring process and the crucial role the Job Description plays.

Job Description – The hub

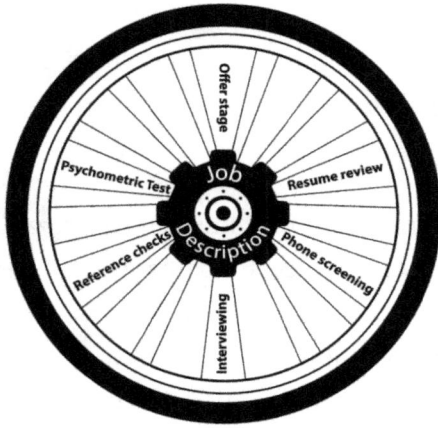

The Job Description sits at the centre of all the steps of a hiring exercise. It's the hub of the wheel. Without it, the spokes have nothing to support them and the wheel collapses.

Of course, there's a caveat to this, and it's that you have a Job Description that works properly. Unfortunately, a great many J.D's don't work as they should.

Be sure to avoid these mistakes

After reviewing hundreds of Job Descriptions belonging to the smallest of start-up's through to listed corporations, I found the majority contained one or more of the three common J.D mistakes.

Mistake one is the J.D which contains every conceivable duty the new employee *might* be expected to perform. It's an excessively long document. The reader usually finds it overwhelming.

Mistake two is the J.D which fails to prioritize the duties of the new employee. The length varies but the result is the same. The prospective employee is left thinking: *Where do I start, and where should I be focusing my efforts (in this job)?*

Mistake three is the outdated J.D which has failed to keep pace with how the job role is currently being performed, or it no longer reflects management's expectations of the job.

The Secret Sauce J.D overcomes these common mistakes, and it works for any job role[3].

It's made up of the following sections with one of its key advantages over other J.D's shown on page 9. To save getting bogged down in detail, you can find the Secret Sauce J.D template on our website as a free download: *www.hiringsecretsauce.com*.

Job Descriptions and Business Plans (The chicken or the egg?)

This book isn't trying to advise you on business fundamentals, however before we move directly into job descriptions, it's worth mentioning that unless you are a start-up venture, it is the company's business plan and organizational chart that should come first and second respectively - and which drive the creation of your J.D's.

Any commercial enterprise (let's call them company's) will have at least a basic business plan or strategy – whether it is written down or not.

The business plan is all about the objectives of the company. Once defined, a basic organizational chart is drawn up to list which job roles would be required in order to deliver on those business objectives.

From the job roles shown in the organizational chart, the individual job descriptions are then created.

In order it is:

1. The Business plan.
2. The Organizational chart.
3. Job descriptions.

---

3. *Of course, to prevent mistake three from occurring, an annual review of the J.D should take place.*

The job descriptions will list the specific duties and functions staff will need to perform in order to deliver on those objectives.

Indeed, the Job Description template on our website is largely about listing the individual duties that will need to be performed.

Once those duties have been listed, we can then identify the mix of competencies (abilities) that will need to be demonstrated by the candidate/employee. These competencies are also listed in the J.D.

Some of those abilities may need to have been learnt or taught (i.e.: academic, trade skills etc.), while others may be partly or wholly developed through work experience.

By taking this approach (placing your business objectives first), you can create *impartial* job descriptions. While it may seem like a small point, having *impartial*, objectives driven J.D's, puts you in the best position to apply the Hiring Secret Sauce method.

It's a very simple, although perhaps slightly cold way of viewing things: *Can this person deliver on the duties and functions we need performed, so that our company meets its business objectives?*

The ideal job description format

Over a twenty-year period, I have progressively refined a job description format that works for every job role, and in every industry. Here is its basic structure (with a completed sample and free template available on our website).

A poorly written job description reduces productivity and effectiveness. Employees need to know what to focus on, and in what order.

The Secret Sauce J.D template is comprised of the following sections:

Company:

Job Description for:

Reports to:

Job Summary:

Hours of Work and Holiday Entitlement:

Snapshot - The Ideal Candidate:

Demonstrated Competencies (Skills and Experience):

Personal Characteristics and Attributes:

Duties and Responsibilities (see following)

Salary Package (competitive):

Incentive Scheme (if offered):

Professional Development:

Job Description template

Job Description template (cont.)

Personal Characteristics and Attributes:

*Duties and Responsibilities: (see below)

Duties and Responsibilities (from the template example)

It's here where the major difference (and benefit) lies between the Secret Sauce J.D format and all the others.

This technique is just a part of the Secret Sauce J.D format – but it is the unique part, so we're covering it in detail here[4]

Here's the explanation on how and why to use this method:

1. Build out your J.D by listing (in order), the primary responsibilities of the role/new employee. Focus on the main 5 to 8 duties and no more. A simple table works best.

2. Next to each responsibility list down (as a percentage), how much effort should go into each item. Convert that percentage into the hours per week it equals (e.g.: for a 40-hour week). Note that the highest percentage duties are arranged at the top of the table, working downwards to the smallest.

Here's an example for a Project Manager:

* For a 30% contribution, calculate 40 x 0.3 = 12 (hrs). For a 5% contribution, calculate 40 x 0.05 = 2 (hrs).

Responsibility	% of the job	= Hours per week
Managing projects using tracking software	30%	12
Ordering and scheduling materials	30%	12
Resource planning and management	20%	8
Budgeting and reporting	10%	4
Liaising with external parties	5%	2
Organizing permits and site access	5%	2
Total:	100%	= 40 hours per week

This approach focuses everyone on what's truly important in the job. Once you're at this point, it's easy to compare the skills and experience of your candidates during resumé reviews, phone screening, interviewing *and* reference checking.

With this simple technique, you have also placed a logical cap on the responsibilities for the new employee. There is no point listing ten other responsibilities, if there is no time available in the working week to fit them in.

---

4. *Method was first published in 2011 on a now defunct website called Ezine Articles. Copyright of the author.*

Of course, you may need to list additional, occasional duties, but you should spell out clearly how and when those extra duties would be performed by the employee.

Analogies, analogies, and more analogies

We've already used one analogy where the job description is the wheel hub, and every hiring step has a direct connection to that hub, just as wheel spokes do.

Yet another analogy is to think of the J.D as the foundation of your hiring exercise – just as you would the foundation of a house.

If the foundation is solid, you can build the remaining hiring steps on top of it with confidence, but if the J.D isn't solid, then you're on shaky ground.

So, bicycle wheels and house foundations. Any more analogies? Well, yes. Just one more, if I may...

The *very best* way to think about your J.D is as a map. When you're trying to find something or someone, you need an accurate map. If your map is just slightly "out" or missing some key details, you could find yourself lost, and so it is with a job description. Having a J.D that is a little inaccurate (i.e.: just a little bit "out"), could mean you employ someone that delivers on the requirements of the job role (as you specified them), but that your business objectives don't get met. In that instance the responsibility would lie with you. Another possibility is that you accurately specify the duties and responsibilities required to meet those business objectives, but you don't correctly identify the characteristics, attributes, and experience a candidate would require to be successful.

In either of these cases, you might find yourself having to re-hire again and again, as your candidate (employee) never quite meets your expectations – or they're performing the duties specified, but it's not resulting in the outcomes you need. It could be a vicious cycle where months or even years tick by.

So, the wrong candidate heading in the wrong direction, or the right candidate going exactly where they need to? Get the map right!

With a map, you will know exactly how to find the right candidate.

The first ingredient in the Secret Sauce is this:

> **Your Job Description is your candidate map. Don't go anywhere without it.**

And last, but not least…

Your J.D is at the core of your employment contract

The J.D is the ingredient that keeps on giving. It needs to form the core of your employment contract[5]. When you realize that the successful candidate was hired on the basis of your J.D, then it follows that their employment contract with your company (and any performance management), needs to be based on performing and delivering the duties and responsibilities contained in your J.D.

---

5.   The job description is a central theme in Chapter 14 (Landing your fish – The offer stage).

As unexciting as it might seem, time spent constructing your J.D will pay dividends over and over again, placing your entire hiring exercise on a solid footing.

A final word on your J.D

You can start putting your J.D together now if you want to, but I recommend you wait until you've finished this book before doing so. You're going to learn a lot about what makes a good candidate/ employee in the remainder of this book – and that will point the way to filling in the various sections of your J.D.

With the J.D format being so crucial to the success of your hiring exercise, we've included our J.D template as a free download on our website.

Chapter 2
Fish where the fish are
(How to find your candidates)

Chapter rating

An easy drive – enjoy!

This chapter is about the many candidates you need to find, so that one of them will become the employee you want. It's also known as the Attraction Stage. The three stages of hiring are Attraction, Evaluation and Onboarding.

Now, I'm sure you're wondering what fishing has got to do with attracting candidates. The answer is, more than you might expect.

Developing a fishing mindset is really the key to attracting candidates. Let me explain what I mean...

Let's consider the main steps to fishing. They are:

1. The right bait.
2. The right tools (fishing rod and reel).
3. The right location.
4. The right time.

For the moment, we're going to concentrate on the core of the attraction strategy – advertising your job vacancy.

When it comes to advertising a job vacancy, the four fishing steps translate as follows:

1. The benefits of the job, and in joining your company (the right bait).
2. Using impactful and effective wording in your advert (the right tools).
3. Which Job posting or networking sites to use (the right location).
4. When your advert is placed. (The right time).

As you can see, advertising and fishing line up very well.

Location is everything

Real estate agents will tell you that location is everything. It's equally true for job advertising and naturally enough for our metaphor – fishing.

In the world of fishing, location is critical. Just imagine fishing in a stagnant pond covered in green algae, versus a clear flowing river, alive with vibrant trout.

Here?   *Or here?*

In the wrong place your advertising response could be literally zero (or very few), but in the right place, potentially hundreds.

Finding your best fishing spots

I'm turning this around a little and beginning with Steps 3 and 4 (the right location and time).

A quick Google search will produce a list of the top job posting sites in your country.

The key point to remember here is that you should check again before each new hiring exercise, because the list does move around a bit. At the time of writing, its Indeed.com for the USA and UK, and SEEK for Australia. So, location is all about this – where do you think your candidates are looking for job vacancies? In other words, which sites are they likely to be found on? When you know the answer, advertise there.

JANUARY

S	M	T	W	T	F	S
					1	2
3	4	5	6	7	8	9
10	11	12	13	14	15	16
17	18	19	20	21	22	23
24	25	26	27	28	29	30
31						

it's about time…

Time is **the** unrecognized factor in job advertising.

At the risk of overdoing the fishing analogies, a person could fish at their favourite location day after day and catch nothing.

Same bait. Same rod and reel. Monday through Thursday – nothing.

Monday | Tuesday | Wednesday | Thursday

But then, all-of-a-sudden on Friday: Bingo!

Friday

There is just one factor determining success or failure here, and that factor is time.

We're out of sync...

Let's talk a little about time and connection as it relates to our daily lives.

We can live in the same town or suburb as one of our friends, but literally not see them for several months. We might even use the same supermarket, gymnasium, or library - it's just that we use those services at different times.

And this can also happen when we place a job advertisement. The specific candidate(s) we want may not be looking on the week we place our advert.

There is no way you can know when the ideal candidate(s) are searching for a job like yours. Sure, some of them might subscribe to job alerts (where adverts are emailed to them), but others don't. Your ideal candidate(s) may just not be looking this week, but an event in their lives the following week could propel them into the job market.

When should you start your job advertising campaign?

This might be a little controversial, but it is the case that many people undertaking entry-level jobs conduct their job search between 9am and 5pm, Monday to Friday. That's right, they search for their next job on their current employer's time.

Those in mid to senior level jobs tend to do their searching at two distinct times – the first is on Friday evening after work, and the second is Saturday or Sunday morning.

In other words, this second group searches on their own time. Of course, smartphones mean they can search during lunch breaks, but they still mostly leave it to after-hours.

Know which group you're after and place your advert accordingly. That is: between 8am and 9am Monday morning for the first group, and between 5pm and 6pm Friday for the second group (and even consider splitting between Friday evening and Saturday morning).

Don't lose your freshness...

Regardless of which Job Posting sites you use; your advert will age within two or three days. After that, it's likely to be found on page five of the search results, or even lower (where adverts go to die). You will then need to refresh or start anew.

The message here is to **spread** your job advert across the small handful of Job Search sites that matter in your region, and then **stagger** your advert over time – ideally a two-to-four-week period. As an example, if you have chosen to use three different job posting/networking sites, place your advert this way:

	Job Posting Site 1	Job Posting Site 2	Job Posting Site 3
Week 1	●		
Week 2		●	
Week 3			●
Week 4*	●		

* During week 4, withdraw the advert placed in Week 1, and freshen up the text.

A quick word about job advertising in print media

It's dead. Don't bother.

In simple terms, every large print advert (costing $thousands), will also be replicated online by the advertiser (for only a few $hundred). Anyone who sees the print version is likely to also be searching online (because they're an active job seeker). Consider print media only if your vacancy is for a senior role. And if you run your advert in print, make sure you replicate it online as well. Get it? We're back to the original point – Don't bother.

Let's do lunch – next month

I've lost track of the times my advertising campaign failed to produce the caliber of candidate I was searching for.

What did I do about it? – I withdrew the advert from circulation, waited two or three weeks, and then placed the advert again. The same advert[6], but this time the right candidate came through. Their answer was typically "I wasn't searching for a job last month".

So, are there particular times of the year that improve your chances of success? There are, but of course your vacancy may exist at any time of the year, and you can't wait too long.

Holidays in the sun *(with apologies to the Sex Pistols)*

Every country has several National holidays and some of them span the weekend. It's well understood by recruitment agencies that advertising at these times yields a proportionately lower response than regular weeks of the year. Even those candidates active in the job market will probably suspend their activities to focus on the festivities. The bottom line? Don't bother advertising during these times.

When it comes to holidays, it's the summer break that matters most.

Many employed candidates who are considering a change of job, will usually put the brakes on their job search several weeks ahead of the

---

6. *In truth, you need to regularly review your advert for impact. If ad response numbers are down, tinker with your advert. Consider new or more impactful bullet points, punchier content etc.*

holiday season, and focus instead on "closing the year out". In short, the better candidates have a sense of duty, and focus on their current job. Once again, recruitment agencies know this, and discourage their clients from advertising during this period.

Once their summer holidays start however, the reverse occurs.

Thinking about a change of career?

Many people use the summer holidays to reflect on their life and career, with a significant number deciding it's time for a change. The two weeks following the end of summer holidays see recruitment agencies inundated with calls from job seekers who are looking for a change.

At the same time, savvy employers know that there are a lot of fish in the water during this time, and they begin casting their bait (placing their job adverts).

It's a great time for you to be advertising, but you should be aware that competition is fierce. More fish – but more people fishing if you will.

Take-away: Don't advertise your vacancy in the 4–6 weeks prior to the annual summer holidays and avoid public holidays. Any other time should be fine.

When your candidate is still in "holiday mode"

A small risk when dealing with candidates on or around the holiday period, is that they're not yet fully committed to making a change.

The idea of a change has appeal, and some will take steps to investigate new job opportunities.

They can be good candidates – great even, but they're not quite in the right frame of mind.

Here's one that springs to mind from not so long ago…

TALES FROM THE VꝚULT

I'm seeing red

At the end of a successful interview...

Candidate: *So, when do you expect the hiring process to be completed?*

Me: *In the next couple of weeks - why do you ask?*

Candidate: *I just want to see if there's enough time for me to fly up and back to Spain.*

Me: *Why?*

Candidate: *Well, it's holiday season in Spain, and I've always wanted to attend the annual tomato festival in Valencia (next week), so I've purchased airline tickets.*

Nothing like getting your priorities right when you're applying for a new job?

This candidate needed to be fully available to attend one or perhaps even two employer interviews – and it's always a good idea to be readily contactable if it progresses to psychometric testing and reference checking.

So, I'd be left explaining why a recommended candidate prioritized throwing tomatoes at other people in Spain, over a new job with this great employer.

This candidate was rejected (gently) "Thank you, but we won't be taking this further" before they left the interview room.

The gentle art of seduction (with words)
— *how to write a winning job advert*

And now we come to Step 2 (we're still working backwards on this one).

Step 2 says: "Using impactful and effective wording in your advert" (the right tools).

I'm just going to say (with modesty) that one of the advantages I have enjoyed over the last 20 years has been through our job adverts.

From day one I invested heavily in making our adverts stand out. The result wasn't only more candidates but better candidates. Quality counts when it comes to advert writing.

Your advert speaks directly to the candidate's perception of the type of business you are — professional or not, focused or carefree, experiencing growth or just hanging on by your fingernails.

Rather than tie this book down with a detailed lesson on advert writing, there is a draft advert using my proven template available for free on the Secret Sauce website.

In addition, I've included adverts I have written over the years which have delivered proven results. They're available in an optional package on our website called: **All the hits.**

Every advert in The Hits package delivered the successful candidate for that particular job vacancy. They're proven performers. These adverts cover a wide range of industry sectors, and of course they're easily adapted to suit your particular company.

> **TIP:** When modifying these adverts, try to maintain their flavor — their style, if you will.

A final word on staying fresh.

There may be times when your advert isn't attracting enough of the right type of candidate. In that case, sit back and cast a critical eye over your advert. Imagine you are the candidate reading the advert. Does it excite you? Would you apply? Pass it on to a trusted colleague or friend. Often a fresh pair of eyes can spot something that could be improved. Freshen up and re-post your advert.

Use the right sized net

The wording of your advert and specifically the criteria you specify, is a lot like the holes in a fishing net. Imagine you're going to place a net across the opening of your stream so that only certain sized fish can pass through, and into, your catchment area.

A net with small holes will only let small fish through it, but a net with larger holes will allow small, medium and large fish to pass through – and in job advertising, you need some volume.

A simple example is requesting a level of academic qualification that may not be strictly necessary for performing your job role. Let's say your Advert/Job Description specifies a University Degree, where a Diploma or Certificate level would do just fine.

Imagine now for a moment there's a candidate out there with the perfect mix of experience, capabilities, people skills and achievements, but they only have one of the lower academic qualifications. They read your advert, realize they won't be considered, - and go elsewhere.

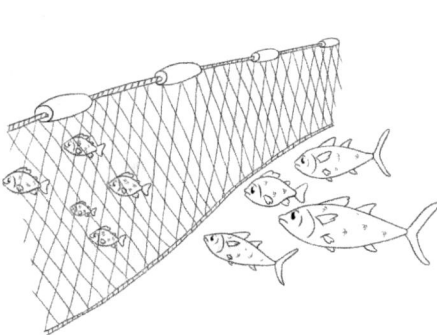

A tight net that stops most fish getting in.   *Or, a larger net that lets many fish through.*

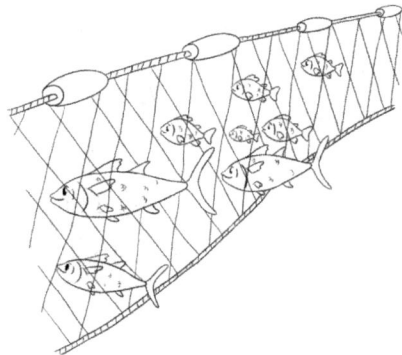

There's no doubt that this approach will result in some less-than-ideal candidates applying to your job role, but it's something you need to go through, in order to find **The One**.

Let them all in, and sort them out later. That's the message here.

Baits that really work

While I mentioned that this book wouldn't tie you down with advert writing lessons, there are a handful of "hooks" that do have a big impact on your advert response (apologies for yet another fishing analogy).

In fact, there are three primary hooks that consistently deliver candidates provided they stack up well against your direct competitors and your broader industry segment.

They are:

1. Interesting job
2. Interesting company
3. Attractive salary package

Sounds obvious I know, but it's a little harder to outline effectively in a job advert. Let's explore these three points:

1. **Interesting job:** There are multiple examples to be found in "The Hits" advert package on our website however, to break this down for a moment, consider that a significant percentage of the workforce desire engaging, interesting and occasionally, exciting work. Wherever the duties and responsibilities of the job line up with the employee's preferences, we find motivated, productive, and loyal staff.

2. **Interesting company:** This second point is tied very closely with point number one. Think about whether you have a growing company or perhaps interesting products and services. If you do, mention it!

Money talks... or does it?

This last point is perhaps less well understood.

3. **Attractive salary package**. It may surprise some readers to learn that money is not a prime motivator for most employees. In fact, money is the prime motivator for only (approximately) 10% of the population.

How important is money really?

The more intrinsic factors of job satisfaction and career growth take precedence. For most people, money is a satisfaction issue. That is to say, most employees look to the money on offer as being able to satisfy their needs, and once that is the case, they look for equivalence with their peers. An example is an employee who checks with a friend performing the same job but in a different company. If their salary package is equivalent to their friend, then they feel satisfied with their level of pay[7].

Naturally, there are exceptions. In different countries and at different times, there can be prevailing economic conditions that cause some candidates to prioritize increased earnings over job satisfaction, but on the whole, these rules hold true.

7. It's known variously as equity (or inequity) theory and is discussed further in Chapter 14.

So, what does this mean for your job advert?

It means you will need to research competitive salary packages for your industry segment, your region, and if possible, your direct competitors. While I do not advocate offering more money than your competitors (starting an arms race over salary), there's no escaping the competitive requirement.

Some background here – wherever I have listed a competitive salary in my adverts, the total number of applications rise by around 40%. That's a huge number. Looking at it from the other side, can you really afford to have 40% less candidates apply to your advert?

Great adverts, then, are the second ingredient of the Secret Sauce.

Spend the necessary time to create a truly impactful advert, and the right candidates will apply.

A final thought to leave you with, on the power of your job adverts:

What is the number one question I am asked by applicants during phone screening? It's the following:

Q. Can I ask who your client is – the company that you are advertising on behalf of?

Every applicant (candidate) wants to bypass the recruitment agency and go direct to the employer.

And why wouldn't they? That's the power of your advertising program – keep in mind that recruitment agencies don't create jobs in the economy. They fill vacancies that are created by employers. If you're rightfully proud of your company name (your brand), then use it in your job adverts.

Chapter 3
Technology screening & evaluation
(Yes, or no?)

Chapter rating

A short drive. This won't take long.

There are a range of tools available out there right now, which can perform a pre-screening function for you.

In their simplest form, these are questionnaires for your candidates to fill in, or aptitude tests to be completed. The next level up are virtual interviews where candidates sit at their computer, and respond to questions asked by software (or A.I if you will).

Still other versions have candidates do a short presentation, which is recorded and viewed by the employer – note that the employer still needs to read through or view these accordingly. Let's look at each type briefly.

Questionnaires – aptitude tests

The questionnaire can be something you produce yourself, or it can be an existing proprietary type where the work is done for you. Aptitude tests are a third-party product that are priced on a per-test (per candidate) basis.

Often, these questionnaires are part of a software program you purchase or subscribe to via an online portal. Try "pre-employment questionnaires" as a google search.

These services can manage your applications, store your candidate resumé's, issue the questionnaires or aptitude tests, and post their results to your portal for viewing. To justify the cost and complexity of these systems, you really need to be hiring in significant numbers each year.

Let's take a quick look at an aptitude test (with scores) for an accounts payable clerk.

Detail Score Report

Q#	Status	Task	Topic	Level	Time
1	Correct	Reporting	Book-keeping	Basic	00:00:58
2	Correct	Overview	Accounting	Basic	00:00:40
3	Incorrect	Calculating Costs	Cash Flow	Basic	00:00:27
4	Incorrect	Recording Sales	Accounting	Basic	00:01:49
5	Correct	Reporting Income	Book-keeping	Intermediate	00:00:57
6	Correct	Journal Entries	Book-keeping	Basic	00:03:10
7	Incorrect	Payables	Invoice Handling	Basic	00:01:39
8	Correct	Procedures	Accounting	Advanced	00:00:36
9	Correct	Approving Invoices	Invoice Handling	Basic	00:02:13
10	Incorrect	Credits	Accounting	Intermediate	00:00:17
11	Correct	Calculating Worksheets	Book-keeping	Advanced	00:01:51
12	Incorrect	Purchase Orders	Invoice Handling	Basic	00:00:36
13	Correct	Reducing Paper Work	Accounting	Advanced	00:00:47
14	Correct	Supplier Disputes	Processes and Procedures	Intermediate	00:00:54
15	Correct	Calculating Discounts	Cash Flow	Basic	00:00:19
16	Correct	Electronic Invoicing	Processes and Procedures	Basic	00:00:49
17	Correct	Purchase Order Procedures	Invoice Handling	Basic	00:00:10
18	Incorrect	Emergency Payments	Cash Flow	Intermediate	00:00:21
19	Correct	Duplicate Payments	Cash Flow	Basic	00:00:21
20	Correct	Supplier Discrepancies	Processes and Procedures	Intermediate	00:01:20
21	Incorrect	Invoice Errors	Invoice Handling	Basic	00:00:24
22	Correct	Trial Balance Sheets	Book-keeping	Advanced	00:02:13
23	Incorrect	Petty Cash	Cash Flow	Basic	00:00:32
24	Correct	P & L Statement	Book-keeping	Intermediate	00:01:02
25	Correct	Eliminating Paperwork	Processes and Procedures	Basic	00:00:56
26	Incorrect	General Ledger Accounts	Book-keeping	Basic	00:00:53
27	Incorrect	Master supplier File	Accounting	Basic	00:00:24
28	Correct	Accounts Payable Functions	Processes and Procedures	Basic	00:00:20
29	Correct	Cash Management	Book-keeping	Intermediate	00:02:46
30	Incorrect	Utility Expenses	Book-keeping	Basic	00:01:49

As we can see, there were several incorrect answers for this individual. Their category totals looked like this:

Question Level Statistics

Level	Number of Questions	Number Correct	Total Percentage
Basic	20	11	55%
Intermediate	9	5	56%
Advanced	5	5	100%
Total	34	21	62%

Question Topic Statistics

Topic	Number of Questions	Number Correct	Total Percentage
Book-keeping	11	8	73%
Accounting	8	4	50%
Cash Flow	5	2	40%
Invoice Handling	5	2	40%
Processes and Procedures	5	5	100%
Total	34	21	62%

Test Description

The Australian Accounts Payable assessment tests the knowledge of an accounts payable clerk or an office associate that has a subsidiary duty in the processing of Accounts Payable. This includes the processing of invoices, purchase orders and cash flow. This test primarily focuses on the basic accounting concepts used in the processing of Accounts Payable.
Assessments for Australian Accounts Receivable and Australian Bookkeeping are also available.

With a total overall score of 62%, you might wonder if this individual should progress to phone screening or an interview.

As it happens, these test results were for an existing employee who, according to their manager, is performing the technical requirements of the role satisfactorily. These are known as the hard skills of a job – bank reconciliations, general ledgers etc. In terms of the soft skills required in this job – the personality traits of enthusiasm, self-motivation, productivity, conscientiousness etc., this employee is rated as very high/ excellent.

But the question remains, was this employee deficient in the areas identified by the aptitude test? Yes, they were, according to their manager, and training was provided to bridge those knowledge gaps. So, this was a case where the soft skills of the candidate/employee were better than their hard skills. You can read more about this in chapter 8 – subheading: hard & soft skills (the yin and yang of good candidates). Spoiler alert – soft skills should be your focus, not hard skills.

Virtual interviews

There are a lot of product and service offerings out there trying to convince you that their contactless virtual interviews or their unique A.I (artificial intelligence) systems can deliver the perfect candidate to you each time.

Virtual interviews can certainly play a role. They are best thought of as an advanced form of phone screening. It's a step up on a telephone screening – and if you can organize it, then you should definitely use something like zoom over a telephone screen, but it still can't match the intangibles - body language cues and in-person dynamics that a face-to-face interview can deliver.

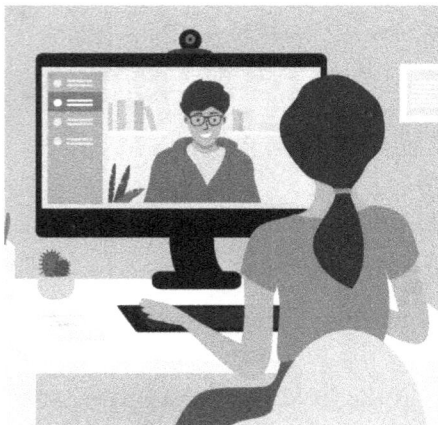

Of the two types available, the self-recorded type with its lack of interaction is the lesser of the two, where a Zoom/MS Teams is better with its real time exchange between both parties.

Talent pools

Yet another service offering is the monthly or yearly subscription for access to a "talent pool" which holds candidates claimed to be pre-screened by virtue of having completed a self-recorded interview.

It's not hard to understand that you're going to see candidates who put their best foot forward in terms of personality, presentation, and enthusiasm for those short few minutes. But does it carry forward to when you meet them in person?

The question then, is are they worth considering? Potentially yes, but only if a monthly fee (with free opt-out) is available. On that basis you could try it as an adjunct to your main attraction methods (your own direct adverts for starters).

The good news is that the secret sauce interview techniques work regardless of whether you are interviewing in person, or over-the-phone/zoom etc.

What's the real benefit here?

These products/services have a place and its mostly in two areas:

The first is where a range of hard skills are essential to performing your job. An example is where you might be hiring a software programmer, and they must be proficient in the C++ programming language.

It could be argued that unless they can program in C++, there's no point considering a phone screen, let alone an interview.

Secondly, there's a benefit if you have multiple job vacancies each year, or you are in an industry where you might expect very significant numbers of candidates. An example could be hospitality or retail sales.

So, using aptitude (ability) tests and other pre-screening tools is fine, and is especially beneficial where high candidate numbers or very special (hard) skills are required.

Even where that is the case, aptitude tests may be better left until after phone screening and interviewing. Why is that? – simply because you might miss some very good candidates if your hiring process is hands-off and automatic. It's a common candidate gripe.

In my experience, great candidates don't like strong technological barriers being placed in front of them before they have connected directly with the employer (a real person).

So once more, if your need is volume hiring, or specific hard skills are required, then at least review their resumé first and conduct phone screening, before issuing an aptitude test.

This gives you the best of both worlds, but ensures you connect person-to-person first.

Keep in mind that a candidate can have the requisite hard skills but fail miserably in the soft skills that make truly great employees.

Hard versus soft skills is so central to great hiring, that it forms an important section later in this book. You can find it in chapter 8 (the good, the bad, and the ugly – people that is).

Interlude – the importance of resumés

Before we leave this chapter, it's worth saying a few things about the value of resumés in the 21st century.

Barely a week goes by where a journalist or employment influencer doesn't write an article claiming that resumés are dead – that hiring via social media profiles or other methods are faster, better, and will somehow yield a superior result. In a way, they're trying to make a case that less is more.

In my view they're missing the central point…

Allowing a candidate (any candidate) into your hiring process without having forwarded a resumé is a mistake. In some cases, it can prove fatal to your hiring exercise or end up damaging your company (and your brand). The reasons for this will become evident as you move through this book, but allow me to just summarize the main issue right here:

By submitting a resumé, the candidate is making a statement about who they have worked for previously, the period they worked there, their duties and responsibilities while there, the skills they claim to have utilized while there, their achievements while there, etc.

You can, should (and will), explore, and then hold them to these statements during your phone screening and any subsequent interviewing, reference checking, verification of qualifications and comparisons to any assessments you might decide to apply.

Evaluation and comparison to a candidate's resumé (content) is the underpinning of every hiring exercise. It all starts with their resumé.

End of interlude

Given that we've been introducing the subject of screening and evaluation technologies in this chapter, it's the opportune time to think about where developments might go next (I mean in the business world and our particular part of it – the world of hiring). Well, that would mean A.I (Artificial Intelligence).

Let's jump in and see what it can do for us...

Chapter 4
We need to talk about A.I
(With apologies to Kevin)

I'm not sure we're truly connecting – yet.

Chapter rating

Set to auto-pilot. You can relax on this one.

If you haven't seen the movie We need to talk about Kevin, it's the story of a boy who, – how can I put this, is indifferent to the mother that created him. The movie is a metaphor for the creator and a wayward creation. It would be fair to say that the mother can't control the son. In fact, it would be more accurate to say that the son is controlling the mother – and not in a good way.

Now, I'm not saying A.I is bad, or that it's out of control. It's too early to make any predictions and, as with all emerging technologies, we can only discuss where it sits today. The real question of course is, what can it do for hiring? The place to start with this is to recognize that some groups think A.I is the future, while others don't.

In researching this chapter, I found three distinct groups:

Believers, Non-Believers and Agnostics. *(Who loves A.I?)*

During my research, I spoke to a broad range of employers and employees. My basic question to all of them was this: "How are you using A.I in your business (if at all), and what are the specific benefits you are deriving from it?"

An early pattern that formed in responses, is that people working in the general business sector are using A.I to help them perform lower-level tasks such as generating sales proposals, assisting with presentations, writing reports, etc. These users regard A.I as relieving them of a few repetitive, or boring tasks.

However, on the receiving end of these proposals and presentations, I found senior managers tearing up and disqualifying said proposals for their "lack of originality, generalizations, and laziness". In other words, many recipients of A.I "products", appear underwhelmed. And for those in the more creative sectors I find they are (unsurprisingly) promoting their individual creativity over a generic feature or method that is available with A.I.

And, for those that regard themselves as experts in their field, I found many are dismissive of the "low-level" responses they receive from A.I chatbots. And of course, there is the majority group – the ones that see some benefit to A.I and are wondering how it might assist them in their business. This last group is keeping an open mind. So, there we have it – our believers, non-believers, and agnostics.

That's all fine for the general business world but once again, we want to know what it can do for us in the world of hiring. Well, the first thing to know is that A.I is incredibly unpopular with recruitment agencies and large employers who do a lot of hiring.

So, perhaps a good place to really start this chapter is the realization that A.I is...

...Working both sides of the room

This is a saying that describes somebody or something that is working both sides of an interaction or transaction. In our case, this relates to the fact that A.I is offering services to both candidates and employers.

Let's begin this by looking at what is available on the candidate's side.

Some candidates are using A.I programs to create their resumé and cover letter. At the moment, I can read through these documents and easily discern the lack of personality between the lines. However, to be fair, I can't call out a candidate I suspect of using A.I to write their resumé without personally interacting with them. And herein lies the clue as to what you will need to do.

The greater the degree of polish within the resumé (i.e.: the further away it is from the real person), the easier your job will be of spotting the discrepancies. The place to find out for sure? – at the interview of course (or perhaps even during phone screening).

Now, of course, an A.I program can't state that the candidate in question has the right type of experience, skills and qualifications required for your job vacancy, but the danger is in candidates who have what you need, and the A.I resumé provides a higher quality of presentation (which both elevates them above their true level, and provides them with an advantage over your other candidates). In the case of cover letters, some A.I programs allow candidates to load in a job advert, and then create a cover letter that will "hit" all the keywords and hot buttons in that advert[8].

Of course, before today, a candidate could always pay a professional resumé writer to create a great resumé for them, but these services are quite expensive which limited their uptake. A.I is free (at present) which means every candidate can get on board.

To some extent then, the issues around fake (or embellished) resumé content, is the same as that outlined in Chapter 7 of this book.

Once again, if there is a substantial discrepancy, telephone screening might be enough to expose the gap between the reality of the candidate, and their A.I generated resumé/cover letter.

Projecting this forward, it's easy to imagine future A.I programs offering interview coaching. So, in time, candidates will be able to access a range of services to help them work on their deficiencies – and therefore, make your job of candidate evaluation harder, but from my experience, the moderate heat that is present in a real person-to-person interview, will always challenge a coached candidate.

---

8. *This is one reason why A.I is so unpopular with recruitment agencies.*

A.I programs are happy to deal their cards to everyone.

Now, let's move on to your side (the employer).

Generic hiring *(A.I will love you - but your candidates won't)*

The term generic hiring isn't an official term – it's just something I call the use of a technology or tool that everyone is using, and where it is predominantly "hands-off". A good example is a candidate who applies to three job vacancies with three different employers - and where all of them are using the same job advertising site. For a bit of extra context, let's assume your company is one of those vacancies, and the other two are your competitors.

Imagine now that all three employers access the same pre-screening questionnaire available on that job advertising site. Our candidate will find themselves answering very similar questions in the same format, and on the same website. By the third job vacancy (let's assume the third one is your vacancy), well, they're likely to be a bit over it. Of course, pre-screening questionnaires are nothing new on job advertising sites, but let's now consider what an A.I version of that might look like.

With an A.I assessment program, all three job vacancies will once again, put the candidate through the program. The difference now is that the process is identical for all three companies – your company, and your two competitors. The other change is that where the pre-screening questions only took a few minutes to answer, the A.I assessment now takes 40 minutes. That's 40 minutes x 3, and the candidate will likely approach it the exact same way each time.

Once again, let's assume your A.I assessment is the last of the three. What's their impression of your hiring exercise (and your company) and more importantly, how do they differentiate your job vacancy from the other two? Has that process done you any favors with that particular candidate? How would you feel if you were in that candidate's shoes?

Placing technology barriers in front of candidates

In Chapter 3, we spoke about good candidates not liking it when technology pre-screening tools are placed in front of them – especially when it occurs before any contact with a real person. So, there is a risk on your side if you go the A.I tools early while your competitor calls your number one candidate and invites them out for a coffee chat. An old saying among recruiters is that "talent doesn't wait" which also means "talent has choices". Time and again, when two job prospects are similar in the candidate's mind, they will go with the proactive, personalized approach – an offer for a coffee and a chat, rather than an opportunity to sit down and be interrogated by your A.I virtual assessment tool.

Good candidates have choices. The personal approach will always win out.

The key take-away here is to ensure that their first contact with your company is via a real person. If you end up using an A.I assessment program, it needs to be after that initial in-person contact – and ideally, after an interview.

Known knowns, known unknowns and unknown unknowns *(with apologies to Dick Cheney)*

If you recognise this statement (by then Vice President of the USA, Dick Cheney), then you would recall that for all the controversy around why he said it, the fact remains that if you work through it logically, it sort of makes sense, although in reality, it can be reduced down to a simpler statement: There are things we know, and there are things we don't know. A.I programs are large learning models. The current versions were developed by having them read millions of books, but they also continue to learn in real-time in part, by what they can grab from you – sorry, I meant grab from your company.

In addition to referencing its repository of millions of books, A.I also scrapes the Internet for the information it wants. Right here, you might be thinking to yourself: if "something" is not on the Internet, then A.I can't possibly know about it right? – well, yes and no.

To better help us understand A.I's abilities and limitations, let's consider an example outside of hiring for a moment.

How much are you willing to share?

I have a contact in the field of advanced materials design. He has confirmed that no-one knows about the work his organization is performing. A search on the internet shows no information on the new metal alloy they are working on, (and this included asking an A.I chatbot). It's too new, and the people involved have an incentive to keep it quiet. What is that incentive? – just the normal position that you don't invest your time, money, and energy into something worthwhile, and then just splash it all over the internet so your less creative, less enterprising, and less hard-working competitors can just pick it up for free.

Just a thought – but you might be similarly protective of the good work your company has done, - along with any I.P that resides within your processes, knowledge base and the particular skills of key employees.

Your business I.P is often your winning hand.

Just relax – and let the A.I vibe wash over you...

Where things stand to get tricky is the point at which you believe A.I can do a better job of assessing candidates than you can, or perhaps when a tool becomes available that you have convinced yourself is an absolute "must have" for your hiring exercise.

To get to this stage, you have to believe that the A.I program is going to be able to accurately assess your candidate not only for their skills, qualifications, and personality traits, but also for their match to your company and to you personally (or whoever the candidate will report to as their manager). And I left out one very important factor – how the A.I program is going to uncover a candidate's true level of enthusiasm and desire to work for your company, as opposed to your two competitors. Not sure? Neither am I, and I'll bet neither is the candidate (at least until they get the chance to sit down with you and learn about your company).

A minimum requirement for all this to happen is for key information on your company to be handed over to a piece of advanced software owned by who exactly?

This information exchange will need to include information on you, because that same piece of software will likely want to assess you as the hiring employer-manager. Are you ready to be assessed down to your personality traits, preferences, and management style (including your performance expectations?). If your answer is yes, are you once again happy for that information to be kept by a piece of software owned by who was it? – and shared out (albeit anonymously, to your competitors). You can be certain this last point will happen because it will be in the Terms and Conditions when you first sign up for that A.I product-service[9].

And let's take this a small step further. It's easy to imagine an A.I program suggesting that if you really want it to do the best possible job for you, why not upload your organizational chart and job descriptions? Once it has those, it can tell you if you're about to hire the right job role, or if it should "adjust" your Job Description for you.

The answer for you and your company might well be yes. You may feel that the handover of information on your side is worth it for a good result/efficiency gain.

Thanks for sharing...

9.   *And that's exactly what I found when I signed up on the A.I software used to research this Chapter.*

Once more, both your organization and your main competitors would access the same programs for this. Reasonably, you might expect similar recommendations and adjustments to all of your competitors' job descriptions.

Are you on your way to sameness, me-tooism and ultimately, mediocrity with no discernible difference? - no key differentiators to make your opportunity more appealing to the preferred candidates you have identified?

Some of the benefits available now with A.I

Certainly, there are some benefits available now with A.I and it's mostly in the area of Job Descriptions. While they fit firmly in the category of "generic", what is on offer out there, could be better than what you currently have. If your organization is lacking in J.D's, then almost anything will be better than nothing.

What A.I will never be able to do for you

There are actually quite a few things it won't ever be able to do for you, but here are the big one's worth keeping in mind:

A.I will never be able to fact check claimed academic qualifications. No University or training college is going to allow a piece of third-party software to access their sacred database – you know, issues of privacy, prestige, reputation etc. Another that fits into the never category are the people you need to call as referees for your candidate (refer Chapter 13). If I were acting as the referee for someone who had worked for me, that discussion will be on a one-to-one basis, and it will very likely be contextual. I'm sure the person calling me will have some very specific (experience, achievement, and scenario based) questions they will want to ask me.

True A.I – Are we there yet?

As of 2025 to the best of my research, all the programs available, do not qualify as true artificial intelligence. That is to say by definition, there are no programs or entities that are thinking independently, thinking for themselves, or producing anything that you and I might recognize as "the next step".

There are no programs or entities out there which are alternatives to humans – experiencing thoughts, dreams or aspirations for themselves. If that day ever arrives, then we might be heading for an entirely different economy and society.

But, once again, that's outside the scope of this book.

Summary:

A.I is presently a productivity and process enhancing tool, making some leeway into candidate assessment. It's a long way (if ever) from replacing the part you need to play in candidate attraction, evaluation and especially, the person-to-person interaction every candidate and employer wants and needs, before deciding to work together.

You could certainly adopt some of the tools being offered if you feel the result is superior to what you could otherwise achieve by yourself.

Is there an ingredient here?

I'm afraid not. At this stage there is nothing in the world of A.I that is unique, or that is in the "must have" category.

But, I'll be keeping an eye on it.

And so should you...

Chapter 5
Start the matchmaking
(Resumé reviews & initial screening)

Ultimately, you will only be hiring one person…

Chapter rating

You're heading off on a long-ish drive. Enjoy!

Now that we've discussed A.I, the reality is that the vast majority of employers are not presently using any form of automated applicant tracking or screening technology. However, even if you are one of those employers that are, you're still going to be receiving applications and needing to engage personally with them (and especially with those you want to perform some initial screening on). So, we're back to the reality of person-to-person engagement.

That exact moment when the first of your candidates apply to your advert, is when your hiring exercise has truly begun. In a moment we'll look at how you actually go about doing "ad response", but for now, let's talk about numbers of applications, and what you might expect. As a guide, let's consider my experience with ad response across 20 years:

Historically, for every 50 candidates that applied to one of my adverts, around 5 were well-aligned to the J.D, and were phone screened.

Of the 5 that were phone screened, only 1 or 2 passed and were invited in for an interview[10].

Of the 1 or 2 interviewed, either or both passed, and made it onto the shortlist.

As an agency, we typically interview between 5 to 7 candidates per job vacancy, in order to achieve a shortlist of 3 – 4 solid prospects. Converting this back to ad response numbers, you can see that your advertising campaign needs to attract somewhere between 175 and 350 candidates. You're possibly thinking to yourself right now - there's something wrong with those numbers and that surely, you could attract just 50 to 100 applications and have around 10 solid prospects. Can you spare a minute while I tell you about my perfect hiring exercise? It went like this:

10. *Successful phone screening is determined by how well they scored using the Hiring Secret Sauce Screening Proforma. This is part of the document set available on our website.*

"I walked into the office Monday morning and was phoned by a new client who said she had heard about my excellent reputation as a recruiter, and was therefore giving me their job vacancy to fill – at our full fee rate.

As soon as I created and placed the advert on our preferred Job Advertising Sites, twenty candidates applied (and only twenty).

I couldn't separate the twenty candidates on paper. Each one perfectly matched the Job Description.

At random, I selected three of the candidates for phone screening. All three passed the phone screening with flying colors.

I subsequently interviewed the three candidates. Following their interviews, they all remained outstanding prospects for the job vacancy. My client, (The Employer) interviewed the three and agreed that they were all outstanding. So much so, that she couldn't make up her mind which one to offer the job to. Reference checking demonstrated flawless work histories. After three days of consternation, a job offer was put forward. During this time the other two shortlisted candidates advised me they were happy to wait, in case the offered candidate didn't want the job (for some strange reason). The offered candidate accepted instantly – no haggling over salary, nothing.

I then woke up – having almost knocked over my coffee".

Every recruiter who hears this story laughs - because they know those big application numbers are real. Sorry.

OK, so it's not a real story, but what is the truth behind those big numbers?

The reality is that many applications will be wide of the mark – some way out wide. You could be advertising for an IT specialist and receive an application from someone who has built their own desktop computer, and now feels your job role is their next logical career step.

There's no doubt that a well-written job advert will reduce some of those wide-of-the-mark applications, but it won't rule them all out.

Keep in mind also, that it's your J.D that includes specific duties, the list of responsibilities, other company-specific requirements etc., and because this J.D criterion is not included in your advert, many candidates cannot know they are not serious contenders for your job role. And to be honest, you really need to keep it that way. Recall that your job advert is the bait, and you want to make it appealing. Job adverts are meant to entice – without overselling the job or its benefits.

I could go on, but I'm sure you get the point. Big numbers are unavoidable, and that's just how you want it.

Excuse my bluntness, but I need to ask you...

It's at this point where things get a little, how should I put it? – direct. Some might say blunt. Whichever way you care to look at it, some hard questions need to be asked.

Candidates will be applying to your job advert using the applicant management tools provided by those job sites. Most will be in the form of resumé's emailed to your Inbox or, you may need to login to their website portal.

Other candidates may call you or direct message you (from certain networking sites).

Through whichever method they apply to your job vacancy, there are just four possible outcomes from now - as follows:

i. Rejecting an application up-front (based on a review of their resumé).

ii. An unsuccessful phone screening (resulting in a verbal rejection).

iii. An indecisive phone screening (keeping the application open for further review).

iv. A successful phone screening (advancing to an interview).

Naturally, you have your J.D by your side as you review, phone screen, or reject candidates – I know, I didn't need to mention it.

Dealing with rejection

I've chosen this heading because what matters here as you begin your reviews, is the sensitive and timely handling of any unsuccessful applicants/candidates.

There are three rules here with a simple and effective process for you to follow:

Rule 1. Candidates are only ever rejected based on skills, experience, qualifications, or preferences – never on anything personal.

Rule 2. Rejection letters are sent out to every unsuccessful resumé review, and they're sent out in a timely fashion.

Rule 3. Any candidate you have spoken to (which you deem unsuccessful) is only ever rejected verbally. They do not receive any form of letter. I'll explain why and how.

For **Rule 1**, there is a very effective, considerate, and impartial rejection letter included on our Secret Sauce website. It's been the mainstay rejection letter in my agency for years.

Rule 2 is important because each applicant has expressed an interest in your job vacancy and by extension, in your company. Receiving a rejection letter[11] may cause some initial disappointment, however by learning of this outcome promptly, it helps the candidate to move on and focus on their other job applications. It's also an exercise in brand management for your company.

By advising them early, any disappointment is balanced by the recognition that you are a professional and considerate company. Each one of those rejected candidates has a view (and increasingly with social media), a voice. Timely and considerate rejections create either neutral or favourable opinions of your company. Late, or worse still, no communication at all, can cause reputational damage.

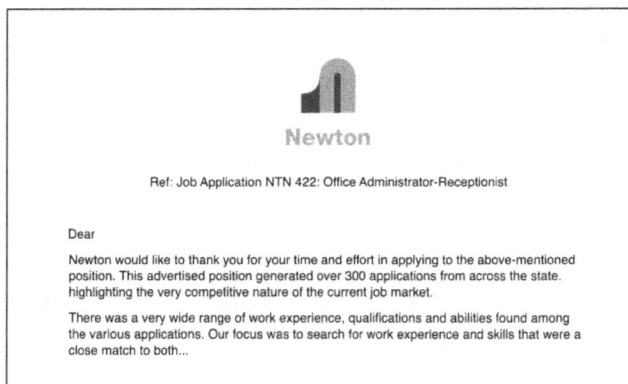

Newton

Ref: Job Application NTN 422: Office Administrator-Receptionist

Dear

Newton would like to thank you for your time and effort in applying to the above-mentioned position. This advertised position generated over 300 applications from across the state, highlighting the very competitive nature of the current job market.

There was a very wide range of work experience, qualifications and abilities found among the various applications. Our focus was to search for work experience and skills that were a close match to both...

Rule 3 exists because any unsuccessful phone screening can be handled in the moment – and that's in everyone's interest. Later in this Chapter there is a basic script you can use. Once a candidate has been either spoken to or met in person, the golden rule is they receive a verbal rejection. It's worth keeping in mind that phone screened candidates may not be perfect for this particular job vacancy, but may have a skill set that suits a future job vacancy you may have. A small investment of your time here via a phone call, could have longer-term benefits for your company.

11.   *A free rejection letter template is available on our website for download.*

A process to follow

Whether this will be your first phone screening, or you've done it before, what you need more than anything else is a script – in the form of relevant questions to ask.

Consistency and repeatability are the keys here. Because phone screening is effectively the first stage of an interview, we're looking for it to advise us whether a candidate matches the requirements of our J.D. If there is a strong match, then the next step is an interview. It's a key part of Hiring's Secret Sauce that the Initial Screening Proforma uses the same format as the Interview Proforma. They are interlocking parts of the "Evaluation Stage" of your hiring exercise.

If you look back to the first chapter in this book, we can start to see the impact of your J.D. It's already helped to create the job advert, now it's underpinning your phone screening. On our website – www. hiringsecretsauce.com – we have included our J.D template as a free download, and our Screening Proforma is available as part of our Professional Series Proformas. This makes phone screening so much easier.

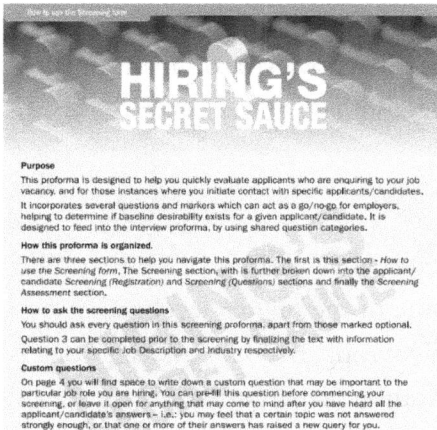

How to use the Screening form

HIRING'S SECRET SAUCE

Purpose

This proforma is designed to help you quickly evaluate applicants who are enquiring to your job vacancy, and for those instances where you initiate contact with specific applicants/candidates. It incorporates several questions and markers which can act as a go/no-go for employers, helping to determine if baseline desirability exists for a given applicant/candidate. It is designed to feed into the interview proforma, by using shared question categories.

How this proforma is organized.

There are three sections to help you navigate this proforma. The first is this section - *How to use the Screening form*, The Screening section, with is further broken down into the applicant/candidate Screening (Registration) and Screening (Questions) sections and finally the *Screening Assessment* section.

How to ask the screening questions

You should ask every question in this screening proforma, apart from those marked optional. Question 3 can be completed prior to the screening by finalizing the text with information relating to your specific Job Description and Industry respectively.

Custom questions

On page 4 you will find space to write down a custom question that may be important to the particular job role you are hiring. You can pre-fill this question before commencing your screening, or leave it open for anything that may come to mind after you have heard all the applicant/candidate's answers – i.e.: you may feel that a certain topic was not answered strongly enough, or that one or more of their answers has raised a new query for you.

Back to that blunt part

Earlier in this chapter I mentioned there are just four broad outcomes once applications start coming in. Let's review them in detail, one by one.

1. Rejecting an application up-front (based on a review of their resumé).

A major aim of the screening stage is to reduce the large number of applicants, until we arrive at those we want to phone screen. The resumé review is the most efficient way of identifying those applications that do not meet the main criteria of your job vacancy.

Referring to your J.D, you should focus on how well an applicant's resumé matches on these six areas:

    i.   Competencies required to perform the job (skills).

    ii.   Specified amount of experience in demonstrating those competencies.

    iii. Achievements cited, and how well they relate to your job vacancy.

    iv. Preferences outlined for your type of job vacancy.

    v.   Preferences outlined for your style/size/type of company.

    vi. Academic or other qualifications specified for your job vacancy.

There are more areas you could consider, however too many areas now will make reviewing resumé's quite difficult and very time consuming.

Let's move on:

2. Unsuccessful phone screening - verbal rejection.

I'm going to begin by outlining some of the higher-level issues which tell you a candidate is very likely wrong, before exploring some of the (fail) answers which are also commonly encountered.

    i.   Top of the list is a lack of enthusiasm for your job vacancy, for your company, for your industry, and well, just a lack of enthusiasm in general. Tell-tale signs of this are shorter, non-expansive responses to your questions. In other words, you tend to get the minimum from this type of candidate.

ii. Closely aligned to point i, is no real understanding or specific desire to be working for your company or industry.

This tends to come across as an indifference to what they want to be doing in their work, or an indifference for the actual job type. You may hear comments such as: "I'm happy to do that type of job" or, "I don't mind working in that industry". What you need to hear is the desire for the job, a desire to be working in your industry or, for your type of company. If it's not there well...neither is an invite for an interview.

iii. I also strongly recommend having some specific "**Must Have's**" or "**Deal Breakers**". Highlight in your J.D and Screening Proforma the non-negotiable areas, skills, and qualifications for your specific job role.

Compromising on your J.D is a major cause of hiring failure. Giving a pass in one or two critical areas (where they don't deserve it) because they're answering most of the other questions well enough, is a mistake.

Remember. Close enough isn't good enough.

Did they really say that? *(the wrong resumé content)*

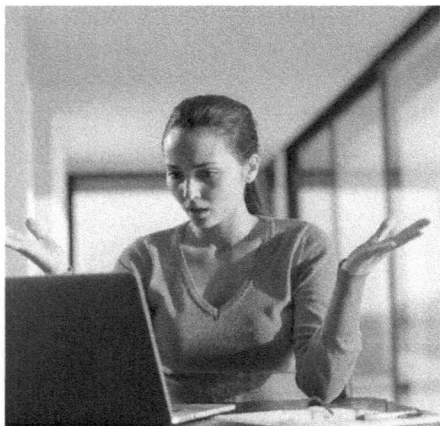

Is it surprising that year after year, the same poor responses to common phone screening questions are heard?

I'm not sure what it is, but they keep coming up. Often, it's a slight variation on the theme, but I've included the main ones here. Clearly, many of these would not warrant a phone screening call from you, so just imagine they are phone enquiries calling to discuss their application. In these interactions, imagine it is you (Q) asking the questions.

Q. Your resumé shows that, on average, you remain with your employer for 14 months. What can you say to convince me that you would stay with us long-term?

A. *I just haven't found a company I really liked. Your company sounds great, I'm sure I would stay long-term.* ✘

Q. We're advertising for a UNIX software coder to work on our maritime navigation system.

A. *Although I've always sold cars for a living, I have written some code to instruct my remote-controlled racing car. Software is a hobby of mine.* ✘

Q. We require a civil engineer to work on a new bridge design.

A. *I'm a mechanical engineer- many of the principles are the same.* ✘

Q. Why do you want to be a Financial Planner – as per our advert?

A. *My university degree (in economics) qualifies me to become a financial planner.* ✖

Q. We have outlined a salary of $60,000 per annum. You have mentioned that you are seeking a salary of $70,000 per annum. Why then, did you apply to our job vacancy?

A. *$10,000 isn't a huge difference. I thought once you met me and agreed I would make a great employee, that your salary package could stretch another $10,000* ✖

Q. Our advert explains that we are a small-to-medium sized company, but your resumé says you are seeking employment in a large, multi-national company.

A. *I did write that, but I'm very flexible. The size of the company doesn't really matter, it's the people that count[12].* ✖

This is the third ingredient in the secret sauce:

> **Be discriminating and demanding in your phone screening. Don't waiver from the requirements of your J.D.**

You might feel that some of the questions in these unsuccessful phone screenings sound a little blunt. They are indeed my words – questions and statements I've delivered hundreds of times over.

Some may find this task a little challenging but if you want to perform effective phone screening, then you will need to adopt a similar approach – you need to be discriminating. It's essentially about probing the candidate - asking them to provide additional details and more corroborating evidence of any claimed achievements.

The good news? – Fortunately, there is rarely (if ever) any form of resentment or "push-back" from candidates that are phone screened. The answer here lies in their recognition that you are offering the job,

---

12. *While this last response sounds plausible, keep in mind that the candidate was either too lazy or not focused enough to tailor their resumé to your advert before sending in their application – and that's not good enough.*

and that an application on their part comes with an expectation of questioning and probing. There's no reason for you to be concerned.

A quick word about faked resumés or untruthful content...

In Chapter 7 (Fake news. Fake media. Fake people), we look at the lies, embellishments and omission of important details that are increasingly found in resumés today. The methods for cutting through those lies are the other steps of the Secret Sauce beginning with interviewing. You may want to jump ahead and familiarise yourself with the basic content of that chapter, before you settle into your phone screening.

3. **Indecisive phone screening (keeping the application open for further review).**

This is where a scoring system really pays dividends. In the Secret Sauce Screening Proforma, each question has a score range between 1 and 5 which indicates how well the candidate answers each of the questions. Mid-range scores are what you would find for an indecisive phone screen. This helps to justify your decision, and it provides for an obvious comparison to your better candidates.

The factors that cause an indecisive outcome are uncertainty of information provided, mediocrity, or hardest of all, simply too early in the phone screening process for you to make meaningful comparisons.

This last point rears its head when you are screening candidate number 7, and there are still 30 resumés per day hitting your Inbox.

Where this is the case, the following phone script can help:

"Thanks for your enquiry and/or forwarding your resumé.

After having spoken to you, I can certainly recognise your particular strengths/skills/knowledge areas. At this stage, it is still quite early in our advertising campaign, and it is our policy to receive all applications first, so we can make valid comparisons between applicants. We then decide who we will be extending an interview to. Whichever way things go, we will be communicating back with you.

I expect our timeframe for this will be around 1/2/3 weeks (as you nominate).

Thank you again for applying to our vacancy."

4. A successful phone screening (advancing to an interview).

This is the reason we're here.

Previously in the unsuccessful phone screening section, I outlined some higher-level issues to be aware of. On the flip side, there are several positive indicators that can point the way to a successful phone screening.

The following points **are in addition** to the candidate possessing the relevant skills, qualifications, and experience to do the job.

    i.   The overarching theme you really need to focus on is **enthusiasm** and **motivation**[13] in the candidate. I can't possibly overstate the importance of this in everyone you speak to, and everyone you interview. I'll cover this again in the Interview Chapter because it's so critical to successful hiring.

          Enthusiasm for the specific job role you are hiring for, and the

---

13. *This also marks the beginning of our introduction to soft skills and personality traits, both of which form a very important component of successful hiring, and which we explore in greater detail in Chapter 8.*

motivation to pursue your opportunity. These are the candidates who want to do the job you are hiring for, and want to be working for your company, and/or your industry.

ii. Closely aligned to the above point is **passion** and **understanding**. In discussion, you'll appreciate that these candidates have a **passion** for your industry – they tend to live and breathe it. For some, it may even be a hobby which they dedicate some of their free time to. An example is a finance person who gets up early each morning to watch the share market in other regions of the world. In short, these candidates have an in-depth understanding of the workings of your job industry, and they know how their skills or experience fit in.

iii. Another key indicator is the ability to answer your screening questions accurately, concisely and with relevance. While this may seem obvious, concise and accurate answering, are markers of a clear thinker, and of a person that is focused on the subject at hand. These traits often transfer into their employment, where we find conscientious employees. Naturally enough, the opposite of this could have been placed in the unsuccessful screening section.

You can use your own J.D and questions to ask in your phone screening, or you can adopt the ones we offer on our website www. hiringsecretsauce.com. Whichever way you go, a scoring system is essential.

Let's assume then, that we're talking about candidates who are scoring 4's and 5's on your 1 to 5 scale (screening questions). Now what?

Very simply, you need to move these candidates forward to an interview.

There is something that is very important here. That something can move you towards finding "**The One**" or if you get it wrong – to missing out altogether.

In a nutshell, it's speed. That is to say, speed of action on your part. Allow me to explain…

If you (the employer) are slow in picking up the phone to conduct your screening, there is a reasonable chance your potential new employee won't be there when you call. They're already being screened or interviewed somewhere else.

Remember our earlier saying that: "talent doesn't wait".

Active job seekers have multiple applications on the go, and talented candidates are receiving phone calls. You can't wait – not even for an hour, let alone a day.

When you have a resumé in front of you that you judge to be a strong enough match to your J.D, then you need to pick up the phone and get started on your phone screening.

If an application has been sitting on your computer for a few days before you decide to act on it, a subconscious signal is sent to the candidate that your company is not very dynamic. The flip side to this (a quick response), tells the candidate you are a proactive, switched-on employer. This moves you up the list in their estimation.

Let's meet – like now

As and when you identify strong candidates during phone screening, you'll need to keep things moving forward. That means onwards to an interview if they are successful. Be ready to advance your good candidates as and when you find them. It's a nice thought to have all your shortlisted candidates lined up for interview on the same day, but it is very unlikely, and you need to be prepared to bring them in for interview one at a time.

You need to make some form of meeting happen and quickly. If that means an initial (informal) chat over a coffee after hours, then so be it. Just be sure to let them know that the coffee chat isn't a substitute for your full interview – that if the "chat" goes well, then the next step is a formal interview. The interview chapter in this book demonstrates the critical importance of a formal interview. For now, it's:

Get on your front foot and get moving. That's the message here.

TALES FROM THE V⚷ULT

Surely, he can't be serious?

I was hiring for a management position in a blue-chip company. The position paid $250,000 per annum - a decent salary in most people's view.

I always enjoy hiring for management positions because they are easier to fill than mid or entry level jobs. The reason for that is simple: at this level, candidates tend to be more professional. They always turn up on time for interviews, and you can generally place more faith in their answers to your questions. At the end of the day, their continued success depends to some extent on maintaining a good reputation.

I had an interview set with a candidate that looked good on paper. So good in fact, that I couldn't wait to meet him. The interview was set for 2pm. We'd already done the preliminary phone screening two days earlier, and his answers were good enough to warrant an interview.

At the scheduled start time I had to check with the front desk. Where was my 2pm interview? At this level, candidates are always punctual or at the very least they will phone ahead if they are running late.

In this instance, I had to call the candidate. Very apologetically, he explained that he accidentally double-booked himself and asked to reschedule for later in the week.

My first instinct was to reject him outright. Against my better judgement, I agreed to reschedule to later in the week.

Unbelievably, it happened again. Once more, I had to call the candidate when he again failed to show up for the (rescheduled) interview. Even more unbelievably, he asked for a third chance. I told him very bluntly that, "at this level, if you can't manage a diary, you simply can't do the job".

At least I avoided wasting an hour of my time with an interview…

Chapter 6
Why pay 20% more?
(Active versus passive jobseekers)

Chapter rating

You're starting to get good at this!

While we are still in the Attraction phase of the hiring process, there is a second group of potential candidates you could pursue.

Our first group (those who reply to adverts) are known as active jobseekers. This second group are known as "passive" jobseekers.

According to some people, this second group are the ones you want. I've never subscribed to that view. Let me explain why...

Are they truly passive?

I'm going to begin by stating that you can't be a "passive jobseeker". That's an oxymoron. You're either seeking a new job, or you're not. The premise behind the passive concept is that an ideal candidate who is not currently looking for a new job, could be enticed to throw their hat in the ring, if only your job vacancy could be presented to them. If we were back in Chapter 2, I'd probably say something about a big lazy trout.

So right here and now, let me just paraphrase. "They appear to be an ideal candidate but are not currently searching for a new job. You just need to activate their enthusiasm for your job vacancy".

In other words, you've got to "turn on" their motivation to consider your job vacancy. **My point is** you don't need to do this unless they are one of only a tiny handful of possible candidates for your vacancy - or the clear standout. Experience has shown that this is the case only very rarely.

Allow me to introduce you to a fabled hiring task that is familiar to professional recruiters. It's when you've been engaged to fill a vacancy for an underwater basket weaver.

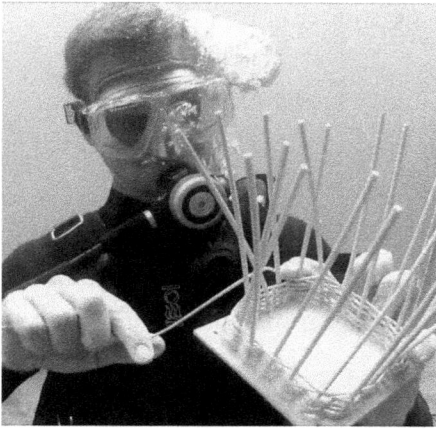

Now, at any given time, most countries have no more than two – possibly three, qualified, underwater basket weavers. If you're tasked with filling one of these vacancies, then you don't bother running an advert, you just locate the two candidates and sit them down for a chat. If you're trying to hire for any job other than an underwater basket weaver, then I submit to you, that there are many qualified and motivated candidates out there, ready to respond to an advert for a good job, with a good employer. Chasing passive candidates has its place, but it's not for the purpose you think. I'm going to bookend this chapter with the how and why on this. For the moment, I'll continue to explain the passive job market, which is also known as "Search".

A bit of background...

The term "passive candidate" originates from the sphere of Search work – known alternatively as "Headhunting". Headhunters keep tabs on candidates of interest which essentially means key personnel in the employ of their client's competitors[14]. Let's imagine that Ford is the client and they're looking for a new Operation's Manager.

For a bit of context, imagine a time before social media and before LinkedIn (if you can). Proper search work involved a recruiter being in

---

14. *Search can be broader i.e.: where you are searching for a new CEO, and they could hail from a variety of backgrounds. For our example, we're deliberately keeping the field narrow.*

regular contact with all the equivalent personnel in the other car companies.

The recruiter for Ford's vacancy sounds out the others for potential interest. It then transpires that the equivalent at Chrysler[15] expresses a "mild" interest. The process of mutual investigation then takes place. Usually very confidentially.

As an employer, you can target passive candidates, and it might work – but it can also come with real costs – both transparent and hidden. Let me expand on that.

Paying 20% more for the same item

There are three basic issues that often come with the passive candidate group.

Let's use one of my own search assignments to highlight the **first issue**.

The following is the approach I use when reaching out to a passive candidate. Of course, I've already identified this candidate (John) as a prospect for the job vacancy. It's just that I can't let him know that.

> *Gary: Hi John. My name is Gary, and I'm an executive recruiter with ABC recruitment agency. I've been engaged by one of the leading automotive manufacturers to hire their new Operations Manager. Although we are only in the research phase of this assignment, your name has already come up a few times as a particularly knowledgeable and well-regarded figure in the industry (flattery).*
>
> *John: Who mentioned my name to you?*
>
> *Gary: I'm sure you can appreciate that all our contacts are confidential – in the same way that I will not be discussing today's conversation with anyone else (establishes trust). I wonder if I could have just ten minutes of your time - if I met you at the coffee shop across the road from your office? There are some gaps in our knowledge regarding lean manufacturing techniques, and I understand you are an expert in this field.*

---

15. *Chrysler is just an example. I'm not suggesting people want to leave Chrysler. Please, (legal team at Chrysler), there's nothing in this.*

This approach may appeal to John's ego and is an indirect way to convince him to meet. Let's assume John meets me for that coffee.

(As an aside, John may innocently mention some of the other "experts" in this field, helping me to further build up my list of potential candidates).

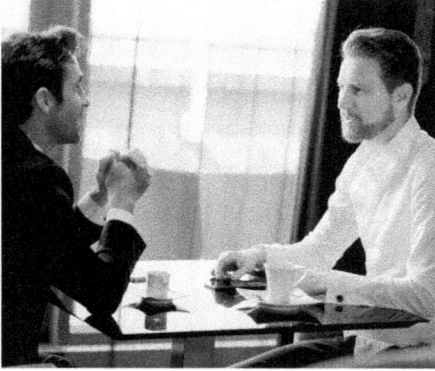

The coffee discussion will indeed begin on that manufacturing topic before I subtly outline the enticing opportunity I am working on.

At some point, John may express interest in the vacancy and begin asking some questions of his own. That is my cue to discreetly ask if this is something that John could conceivably be interested in.

When he confirms a tacit interest in becoming a candidate himself (or at least investigating the possibility further), I feign mock surprise at this unexpected but exciting new development.

*Gary: OK, Well, that's not something I had factored in as I walked over here this morning, but I think I can safely say that our client would be **very interested** in you.*

Allow me to place a call to them today and I will organise for a confidential meeting to take place. This will be in a neutral location – probably outside the city centre and most likely after hours. We need to ensure that the parties are not seen together. It will be purely an informal discussion – an introductory chat if you will. No one at the client company aside from the Managing Director whom you would meet, will ever know that the meeting took place (integrity and confidentiality).

I'm sure you can visualize this coffee meeting scene.

Whether it's John or any other "passive" candidate that has been approached, at the next stage of proceedings, a passive candidate will want to be enticed out of their comfy chair.

This normally means offering them more than their current salary. The typical amount? – on average, it's around 20% more. If they are on a $100,000 salary, our client will need to offer them $120,000. You will too.

Of course, even active candidates who apply to job adverts hope to improve on their salary when they move. The difference is that most will be happy with a small increase – certainly nothing like 20%.

More money then, is the **first issue** typically encountered with passive candidates. Now let's move on to the next most common issue (and it's the one that is most likely to be problematic for your company).

You called me - I didn't call you

If your search exercise is for a professional senior level employee, then you might avoid the **second issue**... but there's no guarantee.

From the previous story, let's skip forward to when you are reference checking, applying a personality profile[16] or preparing the contract of employment.

All too often, passive candidates will ask you to compromise on any reference checks. When they say compromise, they mean skip them altogether. You shouldn't accept this.

Their argument will be that "we" are still in a confidential stage of discussions, and they cannot take the risk that their passive candidature

16. *Personality profiles (also known as psychometric assessments) are discussed in Chapter 12.*

leaks out – it might jeopardise their current employment. It's a difficult argument for you to counter.

To be perfectly honest, news of an imminent move almost always occurs at the point of reference checking, and it almost always leaks out from one or more of the referees.

Some (but not all) passive candidates are going to request that you compromise on one or more of the key components of your hiring exercise, essentially on the basis that **you called them, they didn't call you**.

As you adopt the Secret Sauce method, you will realize that compromising on any part represents a hiring risk, and an opening for problems to occur in your business (and not just with this employee).

Very simply: Do not compromise your hiring process for any candidate.

What you can do

There is a simple practice you can follow, which will prevent many of these issues arising.

Firstly, after the initial meeting with your passive candidate, advise them that moving forward in the process means interviews (likely two or even three), a psychometric assessment, reference checking, and the sighting of any and all documents that support their work history – including where relevant, verified copies of academic transcripts (subject scores).

If they don't agree with all these requirements, then let them walk.

Importantly, let them also know you are continuing to talk to other candidates. It's crucial they understand they are in a competitive situation.

Secondly (assuming they accept your hiring process), is to email them a copy of your job advert and request that they formally apply online. Why? Very simply because it protects your company from accusations of headhunting and more importantly, it helps to reduce (if not completely eliminate) issue two - and hopefully, the following **issue three**.

When the going gets tough, the weak make excuses

Whether or not you compromised on your hiring process to bring in a passive candidate, they can make performance management more of a challenge.

I have witnessed times when an employer has needed to performance manage a headhunted employee. It's not too long before the "you called me - I didn't call you" line is rolled out again. The difference now is that the individual has moved from being a candidate to an employee. If you encounter this… well, it's going to strain relationships very quickly.

I'm not suggesting that this will occur in every case. Where a passive candidate is professional, acts with integrity, and is cooperative at all stages of the hiring process, you can reasonably expect a great hire.

This is about being aware of the potential pitfalls of going down the passive candidate path.

Where passive candidates can be truly valuable – pass it on...

The best way to engage with passive candidates is when you create a networking pool.

Using the example above, I would ask John if it were OK for me to send him a copy of our advert and through this, ask if he would pass it on to other, relevant candidates he knows. I would also ask John for other names – individuals whom I could then approach.

In simple terms, I use approaches to passive candidates as a means to spread the news of our job vacancy. Before long, I start to receive enquiries from good, relevant candidates - ones who are now aware of our vacancy and motivated enough to make the approach.

If John himself is interested in becoming a candidate, he will confirm his interest and perhaps not forward your advert. This is an ideal outcome, as it moves John from being a passive candidate to an active candidate.

Either way, you're up and running with some "passive-active" candidates.

A final word here is about LinkedIn – and I can honestly say that I do not have anything against this particular networking site.

I have experienced occasions where I have approached passive candidates via LinkedIn, and a significant percentage of them have acted as if being contacted meant they were going to be ushered through our hiring process. It's as if by virtue of having created a bio on that website, they are somehow elevated over other candidates. It's as if LinkedIn affords them a special privilege.

These individuals believe that LinkedIn is truly a special place where elite talent resides, and they deserve to be "headhunted" directly into their next job.

I don't know what it is, but it's there.

Just a few minutes into the conversation, and the "Why pay 20% more" maxim rings out loud and true. Once again, for you as an employer looking to hire, these types of candidates have just given you a free glimpse into their personality. Naturally, great candidates can be found on LinkedIn. It's just that the rules of candidate attraction and evaluation are as true for LinkedIn, as for anywhere else – screen them and expect as many unsuccessful as successful outcomes.

Chapter 7
Fake news. Fake media. Fake people.

Chapter rating

Quick and easy.

We've now at the transition phase between locating and attracting our candidates, and the evaluation stage - where we look to go in-depth with understanding who our candidates truly are.

At this in-between stage, we're going to momentarily delve into the on-line world. That place where some candidates give us a free peek at what we might expect if we decide to interview them.

For the moment we're going to separate the various social media sites like Facebook, Instagram, Tik Tok etc., from the professional networking sites. The true social media sites don't belong in this discussion (yet). For the moment, I'm going to refer to LinkedIn and the other, similar professional networking sites.

TALES FROM THE V🔑ULT

All care no care, and no responsibility

Morning coffee. Open my email – There's an invite to connect on LinkedIn from Albert.

Sure, I knew Albert. He was a sales representative where I used to work. I still recall the day he was hired.

The trouble is, Albert's bio on LinkedIn states his title was Technical Manager in the years we worked together.

Er, we never had a Technical Manager at that company and even if we did, Albert wasn't up to doing that job.

As a senior manager in that company, I certainly knew what the organizational chart looked like.

Dilemma: Albert is lying about his work history and is therefore potentially misleading future employers.

Response: Decline Albert's invitation.

Lesson: LinkedIn and every other subscriber-based platform will be the first to tell you it's not their responsibility to vet user content – buyer beware.

In the same vein, let's also consider the case at a US-based web services provider, where an employee was fired when it was learnt he had faked the qualifications on his resumé. The employee claimed to have a dual Accounting and Computer Science degree, when in fact it was solely an accounting degree. Or perhaps, let's consider the case of a newly appointed GM of Strategy for a major Australian retailer, who lasted just one day in the job when numerous "inconsistencies" in his resumé were uncovered. There are similar events going on all the time, and that's enough to say that on the basis of probability, you're going to encounter it at some point.

Who lies wins?

The world has continued to change and evolve, and that's mostly been a positive thing.

However, there has been one societal trend that has been a negative.

It's a trend that led to changes in our Secret Sauce proforma documents. It's a change that has slowly gained momentum over the last twenty years and is conscripting people that traditionally would not have ventured there.

It's the trend of embellishment, the omission of small but important details and in the worst of cases, the obfuscation of truth and the creation of alternative "realities".

In the best possible light, we could say that the ultra-competitive employment market is making some candidates desperate to outperform their competition and "win" the job.

At worst, we could say that some candidates are disregarding the standards and expectations of the people they are dealing with - and electing to lie in order to achieve their personal aims.

My experience is that the reality sits somewhere in-between. The question then is, what do some of these lies look like?

You wouldn't read about it...

I've never made any distinction between a candidate's resumé or their bio as it appears on a professional networking site – and neither should you. The veracity of its content must initially be questioned, and you need to challenge the candidate in order to satisfy yourself of its truthfulness.

I've had a basic philosophy all the way through, and it's best explained in terms of when I'm offering advice to job applicants (candidates). It goes along these lines:

You can write anything you like in your resumé, just be prepared to discuss any part of it in much greater detail and be ready to provide supporting documentation for your claimed qualifications. An employer or recruiter will look to confirm your job titles, responsibilities, tenure and claimed achievements through referees of their choosing.

Regrettably, you're going to have to accept that a lot of this goes on and adhering to all the steps in Hiring Secret Sauce is your best defense and will get you through successfully.

Being switched on early to this phenomenon – i.e.: having a "healthy skepticism" is the best way to go about it.

Fortunately, you can begin very early in the process – such as resumé content...

Let's look at the most common lies I encounter in resumés and bio's. I call them the "**Dirty Dozen**".

1. No longer working there (may have left two months or even two years ago).
2. Did work there, or still working there, but for a shorter tenure than they claim.
3. Never worked there (often a short tenure placed between two real jobs).

4. Claimed they were employed on one or more short term contracts, when in fact they were fired from those companies. (a difficult one to uncover).

5. Worked there, but not with the elevated job title claimed – i.e., was a sales representative, not the sales manager as they claim.

6. Did not achieve the claims they make for themselves (i.e., increased sales by 70% each year for four years). Perhaps it was more like 10% each year?

7. Qualifications embellished or faked – re: the US-based web services provider example.

8. Claimed to have direct reports, when in fact they had none.

9. Claimed to report directly to the GM or CEO, when in fact they were reporting to someone one or two levels below that on the organizational chart.

10. Claims to work in a company of 50 to 100 employees, when in reality, it is a small company of 5-10 staff.

11. Claimed additional responsibilities that either did not exist or were exaggerated i.e.: responsible for sales to export markets, where the company only ever made two export sales in their ten-year history.

12. Claims to be on a salary of $100,000 per annum, but in fact, is on a salary of $70,000 per annum.

Naturally there are more, but I just liked the sound of The Dirty Dozen!

Unlucky number 13 – because I just couldn't stop at 12!

Later in this book is a series called Interview Masterclass. One of the classes is "Expansion questioning". There we take a dubious candidate claim, apply our technique for testing its veracity and essentially, expose a lie.

However, while we're still in the resumé review stage, there is a particular type of candidate that we'll call Unlucky Number 13. This type of candidate manages to combine several of the Dirty Dozen lies in a way that would make your phone screening (let alone an interview), quite challenging. That's because they're adept at obfuscation and double-talk. Let's look at this real-life example (lifted from their resumé), to illustrate the point:

*"**Promoted to general management role** in just two months, after rapid-fire successes in fulfilling the brief to establish a new presence in Northern England. Leveraged the power of quality, established contacts to source high-level staff, and jump-started revenue generation".*

But wait, there's more...

*"**Grew business in a depressed local market** by exploiting international client networks. Acquired new multinational clientele and created new channels".*

And finally, just to cap things off:

*"**Transformed underperforming sales team** to achieve record-breaking sales and contracts".*

Wow! Aside from it all being complete gibberish, notice how none of the claimed achievements are quantified (no numbers or figures next to them). All six pages of this particular resumé contain more of the same. In a phone screen, interview or reference check, you wouldn't know where to start, because every single statement requires clarification, expansion, detailed examination and finally, corroboration by referees – if it ever got that far.

The answer? Don't even bother with these types of candidates. It's always a dead-end.

Uncovering the truth.

The combined steps of interviewing, reference checking, psycho-metric testing and the sighting of qualifications, work together to uncover inconsistencies in the competencies, achievements, employment history, personality traits and qualifications of your preferred candidate(s)[17]

In some instances, lies are uncovered during interviewing, and the candidate is rejected at that stage. With more skilled liars, it might be in the latter stages of psychometric testing, reference checking etc., but they will be exposed.

You can have confidence in being able to identify and reject liars using the methods outlined in this book, in conjunction with the various Secret Sauce proformas on our website. You will need all the tools to do this successfully.

Further in this book we examine one of those lies in an interview setting. Up to this point, there was more value in focusing on what can be uncovered in resumés and bio's and rejecting those candidates at the resumé review or phone screening stages.

---

17. *Most of these steps are applied to the preferred candidates – sometimes known as the "shortlist". A couple of the steps are reserved only for the candidate you intend to offer the job to.*

Chapter 8

The good, the bad, and the ugly

(People, that is... with apologies to Sergio Leone)

Chapter rating

Cruising.

Let's talk about people. What they're really like. That could include you and I but that wouldn't be fair because we're both nice, interesting, engaging, and fun people, aren't we? It's just everyone else we're concerned about.

You and I really do need to be separate from this discussion because it's you and I, evaluating "them". We want to know if "they" are the right people for our business and whether we believe we can work with them. To do that, we've got to understand what makes a good person and especially, what makes a good employee[18].

Fortunately, there's just enough science around to help us with that. Not hard science, but what's referred to as the social sciences. In keeping with the overarching theme of this book, we need to be able to identify the kind of people who are wrong for our purposes, so we can filter them out and advance the people that are right for us. Sounds logical enough!

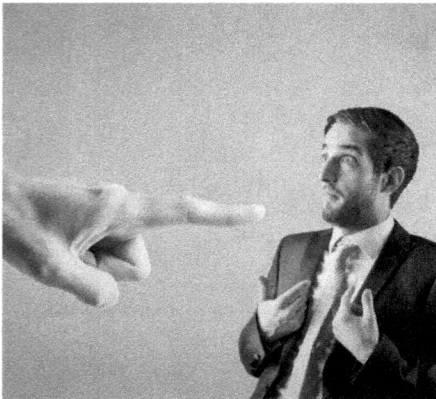

Before we get to the subject of interviewing which is part of the "Evaluation" stage we need to better understand our subject matter - people.

18. *Different personality types may be required to perform different job roles. More on this later.*

Different personalities or the wrong personality?

When we talk about people, we're really talking about their personalities. "Everyone's different" is a common saying. But are they really – different, that is? Because to believe that, is to believe that everyone is unique. Our fingerprints certainly say we are unique, but our personality traits say otherwise.

The basis of our personality is that we all display characteristics (traits) that can be measured and understood, and these traits drive our actions both in our work, and our personal lives.

There are five high level personality domains (or categories) that are universally accepted due to the large amount of research and validity work put into them by psychologists.

Those five personality domains are known by the acronym **OCEAN**. They are:

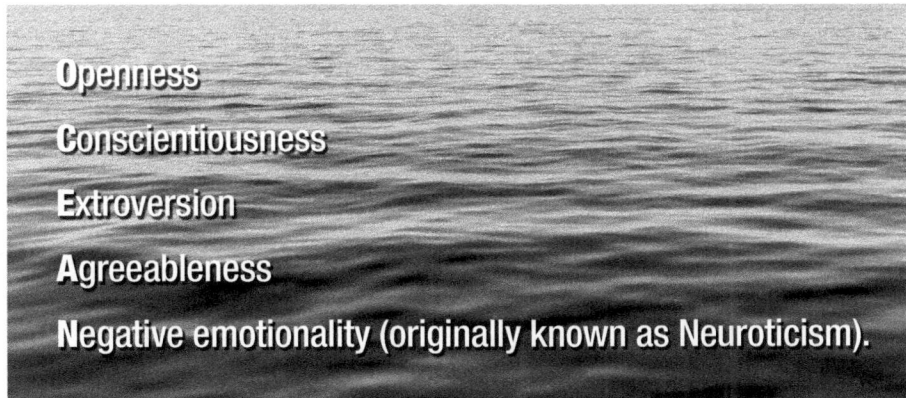

Openness

Conscientiousness

Extroversion

Agreeableness

Negative emotionality (originally known as Neuroticism).

These five major personality domains are each made up of three smaller facets. In total, it gives psychologists fifteen (15) personality facets to work with. In the world of Hiring-Recruitment, organizational psychologists regularly work with these fifteen facets. All of us display greater or lesser degrees of these fifteen personality facets.

As a result, people are different, but many can be broadly grouped together or be recognised for their dominant facets/traits.

The importance of personality traits is that they are good predictors of workplace performance – not just in how a candidate might approach individual tasks or goals, but how they are likely to interact with their colleagues or your customers. The field of testing for these personality traits is known as psychometrics.

On the Hiring Secret Sauce website, we have a recommended psychometric assessment that is a useful adjunct to the other Secret Sauce steps. The appropriate time to apply a psychometric assessment, is after the interview, but before reference checking. This is because a psychometric assessment can uncover new information which can then be confirmed via individuals who have worked with the candidate. In the majority of cases, the psychometric assessment (report) tends to confirm the findings of your interview.

At the very least then, it is a useful confirmation step and, in some instances, will uncover new information. For their low cost, simplicity of use, and our twenty-year history of using them to successfully support hiring exercises, they are a key part of the Secret Sauce method.

Let's now look at the role personality plays in our Good, Bad and Ugly candidates:

They walk among us (not the undead, but the uncaring...)

A lot of people say they have a good BS sensor (BS stands for Bulls--t). Lies, in other words.

I'm not sure how good my BS sensor is, but years of hiring has given me a finely-tuned AH sensor. AH stands for A--hole.

And it's not just that I encounter big egos when hiring executive jobs, although that's often the case. No, I've encountered a--holes when hiring all different job roles.

Fortunately, most announce themselves in strikingly similar ways. They are therefore easy to identify, which has made my job of quickly culling them and preventing them from damaging my client's company all that much easier.

Full disclosure - I do relish my encounters with them. It's more than just a distraction from the mundane (although that's certainly a part of it) rather, I like to think of it as an opportunity to do some good – helping my clients to avoid a poison personality - because that's essentially what they are.

And I can tell you that with very few exceptions, most of the a--holes are males. I suspect most female readers would agree with my observations on that.

Let's be a little more scientific about this. Many readers would regard these types of candidates as narcissists. Referring to them as narcissists is a well-used (perhaps over-used?) term. Where does narcissism fit within the **OCEAN** model mentioned earlier?

Well, it's a perversion of **E**xtraversion, combined with the more undesirable traits of **N**euroticism, and low levels of **A**greeableness.

Its origins hark back to Greek mythology where the young Narcissus saw his own reflection in a pond and was so enamored and fixated, that he eventually withered, died, and then fell into the pond where he was turned into a flower.

Portion of "Echo and Narcissus", by John William Waterhouse, 1903.

The more modern Webster dictionary defines narcissism as: "Extremely self-centered with an exaggerated sense of self-importance". While a lot of that fits, it's still not the whole story. Other key facets we must include are being socially assertive/aggressive, lacking empathy for others, and having little to no conscience. The latter includes taking extreme or even obscene actions and being unwilling to accept personal responsibility for any negative consequences arising from those actions.

We then get the main traits of a narcissist which coincidentally fit perfectly with what most people would recognise as an a---hole. Earlier on I referred to them as "poison personalities". Why don't we take a look at an encounter from 2017 which contains themes covered back in Chapter 7. This report extract covers my interactions with a candidate known as Jonathon. The employer (MGE Electricity) knew of Jonathon and requested that I interview him. I advised my client that Jonathon would be subject to the same process as every other candidate we might identify. The employer agreed.

TALES FROM THE V🔒ULT

10 out of 10 for narcissism.

The following are excerpts from the report I prepared on Jonathon, combined with some of my recollections from that time.

My initial contact with Jonathon was by telephone. I offered to meet casually to explain our hiring process, and how we would manage his application. I explained that mutual confidentiality is assured, and as a part of this, he would be required to apply to our advert. (This would keep MGE at arm's-length, while establishing for Jonathon that he will be part of a transparent and competitive process).

This was met with an unusual response from Jonathon.

He attempted to control the discussion, requesting that I go to him for the introductory chat. He was also not keen to apply to the advert, asking if I could waive this requirement.

This initial discussion gave the clear impression that Jonathon wanted to be headhunted directly into the role. This presents a range of potential issues, the least of which is performance management (should he be hired) where a "you called me" attitude can manifest. The call ended with no outcome agreed.

After several hours it obviously became clear to Jonathon that I was not going to accept his demands, and he subsequently contacted me, agreed to meet (at a central location), applied to our advert, and agreed to fall in line with our hiring process.

Subsequently, I was able to interview Jonathon in our offices.

That's when things really got awkward…

The interview.
The interview began with Jonathon moving his chair to an oblique position, instead of the clearly placed starting point of directly opposite. He insisted on maintaining this position for the entire 80-minute interview, even though it was obvious to him (and myself) that he should move back to the (directly) opposite position.

Explanation: Sitting directly opposite on a round table establishes and reinforces equality between two people[19]. Moving his chair around was an attempt to encroach on my personal space. His hope would have been that I then moved my chair around so that once more, we would be sitting directly opposite each other. Jonathon would then have established a mental edge (I maintained my starting position to deny him this).

Beyond this, Jonathon spoke over me several times, often by raising his voice sharply until he ensured I was cut off.

I allowed him to do exactly that, opting instead to reduce his body language score each time on my interview proforma.

Moreover, it was difficult to keep Jonathon on topic. He is prone to drifting on answers, and segueing into anecdotes to showcase his industry and product knowledge.

Throughout the interview, Jonathon adopted a casual, laid-back posture.

All these body language cues are of a person that hopes (or believes) they can establish a greater-than-equal or even a dominant position over the interviewer – along with bringing an air of superiority.

In isolation, these actions would be sufficient cause for concern. In practice, they reinforced my initial telephone contact (where Jonathon requested that I meet him near his office early in the morning). In other words, he would be controlling the relationship.

Toward the end of the interview, I outlined his high job mobility and asked how he would respond to an assertion of consistently short job tenure.

He was aware that it would be a concern but offered no guarantees for the future.

If we assume that Jonathon's current job search is successful, then he will be in his eighth job since 1997. This equates to an average tenure of two-and-a-half years per job, over the last twenty years (1997-2017).

---

19. *We explore this type of behavior in greater detail later in this chapter.*

Summary

If I were reviewing Jonathon's application without any prior knowledge[20], I would have difficulty getting past his high job mobility[21].

At the heart of the issue was Jonathon's personality and the approach he took in our interactions. Openness and cordiality on my part, was met with mind games, one-upmanship, and a clear desire to impose his will and control discussions.

The core question is this: should Jonathon be representing MGE in the marketplace?

If we combine his high job mobility with his lack of emotional Intelligence, then my answer based on the evidence thus far would be no.

Jonathon's performance saw him register (comfortably) as the ugliest candidate I have encountered over the last 20 years.

Jonathon is an extreme example that anyone would recognise as being wrong, and his narcissism was on open display.

However, many of these types of candidates will be less overt at interview, meaning that their shortcomings will only be uncovered when psychometric testing and reference checking are performed.

Fortunately, there are some other clues you can follow before those stages...

The subtle shades of badness

Referring to our OCEAN model, it's clear that Jonathon would have scored low for respectfulness and empathy for others. These are facets of **A**greeableness. He also appeared somewhat volatile – a facet of **N**euroticism. And while he was clearly an **E**xtrovert, he took assertiveness and social dominance to extreme levels.

Bad candidates aren't bad because they lack the knowledge or ability to perform the job, rather, they're bad because of their personality and

---

20. *Meaning that, without being referred directly by the client (employer), Jonathan's excessive job mobility would preclude an interview invitation.*
21. *While not specifically highlighted in Chapter 5 of this book, a pattern of high job mobility (i.e.: multiple tenures of approximately two years), should be a major concern and a valid reason for rejection in your candidate applications.*

the manner in which this can negatively impact your business, and your other staff.

So, what are the other signs of these bad candidates, and how can you uncover them before it's too late?

Well, social dominance (or an attempt at it), is a major sign. And here is the right time to look at the body language that points to social dominance.

Your body just told me everything

This book is not about teaching you body language. You can find that anywhere.

Our few examples are just those body language cues which are synonymous with bad or ugly candidates.

For example, in most places around the world, mutual respect is a given. This is particularly true when we're meeting someone for the first time – such as in an interview.

As the employer, you are the one with a potential job to offer. Why then would any candidate show you anything less than total respect? – well, some of them won't and that's just the way you want it. Let me explain...

Your very first interaction will likely be via a handshake. That handshake needs to be neutral (or balanced) like this:

Notice that their bodies, arms, and hands are spaced equally apart. Their forearms (including their elbows) are horizontal. That's neutrality, and that's mutual respect. There also needs to be a smile. No smile usually means no personality (or a dysfunctional personality).

Any attempt to cross the imaginary centre line between the two of you is an attempt to encroach on your personal space. This includes if they place their other hand on your hand, your elbow, your shoulder or wherever. It's an attempt at social dominance. This holds true even if they deliver that maneuver with a smile.

Secondly, and undoubtedly the worst of the social dominance attempts is this:

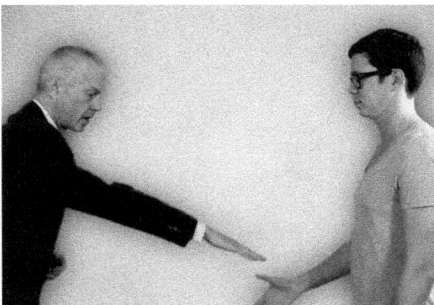

Rather than extending their hand in friendship (vertically) and treating you as an equal, they offer a palm-downwards hand. They hope (as shown above) that you will supinate your hand (turn your palm upwards) and clasp their hand. They have then achieved social dominance over you. It's the act of an a---hole. It tends to be a learnt behavior - for example, their father taught them to do this as a child and they maintained it into adulthood. For all the female readers out there, I can once again say that when I encounter this, it is overwhelmingly with males[22].

My personal response is to twist their hand to the vertical (neutral) position, but I don't recommend you try this. Rather, just note it down[23].

As we progress to sitting down and commencing the interview, we're looking for a candidate that sits upright (perhaps even slightly forward) to demonstrate they are attentive. And, unlike our example of Jonathon, they won't talk over you[24].

During the interview, look for the times when the candidate is discussing their competencies or key knowledge areas. Their position in their chair should remain neutral/normal. You don't want to see the following, or any variation thereof:

---

22. *If this is you as the employer – well, I'm sorry, but it's never too late to change.*
23. *The Secret Sauce Interview proforma includes scoring for body language.*
24. *If they do talk over you – on more than two occasions, subtract another point.*

If you do, then it's a symbol of their (perceived) superiority. It's not social dominance, but it's almost as important. From personal experience, you've also likely encountered a candidate who may be more of a talker than a doer, but let's leave those assessments to your Interview Proforma. We're still focusing on undesirable body language cues.

If you encounter this laid-back, casual approach to the interview, then you need to make another note on your form. Subtract another point for a casual or superior attitude.

While the Secret Sauce proforma contains separate body language scoring, if you're using your own interview questionnaire, then you should also run a scoring tally based on a five-point scale. If your candidate's general interview performance was good but they make all of the (above) body language faux pas, then the maximum they can score is two out of five. Any swearing or inappropriate language? – subtract another point.

The key reason why I suggest merely observing and recording these bad body language cues (rather than intervening) is **ingredient four in the Secret Sauce.**

> **SECRET HIRING'S SAUCE** Make your candidates as comfortable as possible, at all times. They will then speak and act to their true self.

I used this ingredient with Jonathan, and it worked perfectly to expose his poison personality.

We are who we really are, when no one is watching

What we do in the shadows...

Psychologists will argue forever about whether nature or nurture matters more in determining the person we ultimately become, and whether the expectations of society force us to act differently than we would prefer to. The ancient Greeks pondered this very question. Their frame for the debate was whether a "good and honest man" would behave differently if, well, - if no-one were watching him.

And so was written the story (a parable) about the Ring of Gyges by the Greek philosopher Plato.

Gyges was a shepherd charged with tending the King's flock. One day there was a mild earthquake which uncovered the entrance to a cave that had been hidden away up to that point.

Inside the cave he found the skeleton of a giant seated on a throne. Gyges left everything as it was, except for taking a jeweled ring from the giant's finger.

Gyges noticed that by twisting the ring a certain way, that it made him invisible. Astute readers are probably thinking they've heard this before in the Lord of The Rings books.

The short version of this story is that Gyges uses this power inside the King's court. While invisible, he seduces the Queen, ultimately kills the King, and then assumes power. That's one heck of a turn from being a good and honest man.

The Ring of Gyges parable really says this: "We are who we really are, when no-one is watching"

So how does this view translate into the modern world, and does it have a place in hiring?

Before answering that, let's also consider an age-old tradition still used today in parts of Europe, where two people intending to form a business partnership will head out to a restaurant to "get to know each other".

A substantial meal is accompanied by an even more substantial amount of alcohol, as the two budding partners attempt to find out who they're really about to hop into bed with.

It's that old Latin saying of "In Vino Veritas" (In wine, the truth). Having a few drinks is universally accepted to be a social lubricant. Some of the barriers of polite society come down, and things are said that we normally might not say – whether it's outing our political views, commenting on societal trends etc.

What's this got to do with your job candidates? Well, I'm not suggesting that buying a few rounds of drinks should become part of your hiring process, but there is a place where you might be able to see what they really think about certain topics.

It's that fraught world of social media. I say fraught because unless you know what you're doing, it's just as easy to draw the wrong conclusions as it is to learn something "hidden" about one of your job candidates.

Facebook or faceplant?

Social media is about fun interactions with your friends - sharing news, photographs, and stories of interest. However, some people just can't help but push their views on their friends and the broader audience. Whether it's their politics, affiliations, or personal commentary on a current event. And if they get it wrong, it's a faceplant that's hard to shake, as the Internet has a habit of keeping content alive for years.

Many employers research candidates via social media and then draw conclusions based on what they see and read. I've always urged caution with this.

My advice is not to concern yourself too much with a candidate's politics or beliefs, unless they cross into the realm of unacceptable behavior - or views which are contrary to the workplace laws of your country. Of course, everything is subjective, and your opinion of what constitutes good taste is yours alone.

I would recommend focusing instead on how you regard their online personality using the OCEAN model above. Do they appear **A**greeable, and do they display **O**penness?

Extroversion is great, providing they do not appear domineering, or seek to influence others (unduly) to their point of view. Look for a considerate, balanced individual who certainly approaches life with enthusiasm and vigor. All good traits to have in your employees. In short, do their on-line traits match their in-person traits?

So, what makes a good candidate?

At the beginning of this chapter, we used the OCEAN model of personality to help us identify "Ugly" and "Bad" candidates. Naturally enough, that same personality model can help us identify "Good" candidates. In the Facebook example above, I suggested you look for candidates who were **A**greeable – work well with other people, and that displayed **O**penness (creative thinking and ready to try new things). To that we should add the **C** in OCEAN for **C**onscientiousness.

Conscientious employees readily apply themselves to the task at hand, delivering results with a quality focus. And of course, we said that healthy **E**xtroversion was a good thing (bringing a zest for life). Naturally, not all of us are Extroverts (most of us sit around the mid-point - neither clearly extroverted nor introverted) and just to be clear, there's absolutely nothing wrong with being Introverted. Introverted people can and do, make significant contributions to their employers, and enjoy great interpersonal work relationships.

So, "Good" candidates are just the same as "Good" people, aren't they?

Well, to a large extent, yes, they are. And bringing in good people is the only way you can maintain a truly productive, positive and harmonious work environment over the long term.

Good candidates (good employees) are a major underpinning of high retention rates (low turnover of staff).

So, we can clearly define "good" candidates using the OCEAN personality model.

But is it just "good" people we want? – because business is about effectiveness and results. Is there something more that is needed?

As a businessperson or manager, you want to hire the best staff, so that you can gain a competitive advantage over your business rivals.

This brings us back to the statement on the rear cover of this book – that only 10% of people (on average) make things happen.

The 10% typically come with a few additional personality traits – namely: Competitiveness, Drive, and Ambition. These are some of the additional facets that make up the OCEAN model.

If you look back to the Job Description format on page 8 of Chapter 1, it contains this important section: *Snapshot – The Ideal Candidate.*

What if the ideal candidate (a "good" person) actually means a highly driven candidate? A candidate who, if hired, performs at an above-average to elite level for your company – and delivers the results you seek.

Now, what if that candidate places the achievement of goals above the feelings of colleagues? How would that sit with you?

In my experience, the 10% are - how should I put it? - "focused".

It may well be a balancing act that you need to perform if you're going to hire "the best" for your business.

Hard & soft skills. (the yin and yang of good candidates)

Back in Chapter three, we briefly introduced this topic, when we spoke about technology pre-screening tools.

Hard skills are best thought of as **learnt or taught**. As an example, carpentry is a hard skill, along with software programming, engineering, medicine etc. It must be taught to the person, and you learn it through a combination of academic lessons and "doing" (practice).

Carpentry. It requires a lot of practice to master it.

Soft skills are for the most part, inherent to us. They're part of our personality. We are mostly born with our soft skills, although some can be developed (to a moderate extent). This again takes us back to the

OCEAN personality model. Many of our soft skills can be thought of in terms of our traits. Examples here are our tendency towards being well-organized, our level of productivity, being calm under pressure, and our preference to be around, and work with, other people.

Just these few examples tell us that we obviously need to focus on both hard and soft skills in our candidates (future employees).

Just having one or the other set of skills won't cut it, but what we need to say once again, is that hard skills can be taught, but soft skills cannot.

I'm going to say right here, that I have always hired on the strength of the candidate's soft skills, providing the knowledge (hard skills) for the job already existed, or could be easily taught by the employer.

Allow me to take the easy way out here by using the example of sales. Unless we're talking high-end medical equipment, you can generally teach a new salesperson the key features and benefits of your product / service, but what you cannot do, is teach that salesperson how to be proactive, conscientious, well-organized and responsible.

You guessed it. **Soft skills are the fifth ingredient in the Secret Sauce**.

Repeat after me –

> **HIRING'S SECRET SAUCE** — Hire on soft skills. Hire on soft skills. Hire on soft skills.

A quick word about EQ

In short, there is something recognized among the general public as EQ, however a Google search will quickly demonstrate there is no consensus around what constitutes it (EQ), or how someone might go about utilizing it in the workplace. You can't test for it in the same way as you can test for IQ. The closest we might get to EQ are certain facets of our OCEAN model – specifically Agreeableness with its facets of empathy, politeness, respect for others and being non-argumentative. In addition, we might add the **Extraversion** facet of sociability. There's also a small amount of **Open-mindedness** – its facet of curiosity (or interest in new things). But that's about it – it's all explainable inside the Big Five personality model, and without an agreed method of testing or applying EQ in the workplace – well, we're much better served by our Soft and Hard skills approach to hiring[25].

Don't think outside the square – think outside the circle!

The earlier topic was titled "So, what makes a good candidate"? and we followed that with the recognition of Hard & Soft skills. But there's one obvious question we still need to ask here: "Where do you find these good candidates"?

Well, Chapters 2 and 6 focused on advertising or conducting some form of search work to bring them into your orbit. That's still the case, but what I'm really asking here is: from which backgrounds do they come from? Where would I find them if I went looking for them?

When I ask this question of employers (where should they come from?), I usually get one of two answers as follows:

1. From one of our competitors so they can "hit the ground running", with no training required on our part or,
2. From outside our industry so they are fresh and don't bring any "baggage" with them.

So, what they tend to be saying is: "I need someone from either inside our industry, or completely outside our industry".

I've always had an issue with the first option. It rarely brings any excitement for the candidate (e.g.: last week I was selling Brand A, and this week I am selling Brand B). I find the glue is weaker for these candidates and the company. Motivation and enthusiasm just seem to be lower.

25. *Also consider a Big Five based psychometric assessment to help you understand a candidate's personality.*

As a long-term hiring strategy and business model, it's a little fragile in my opinion.

Of course, option two also brings a potential risk - whether the candidate will enjoy working in a new industry. It's an unknown for both sides, but in the case of an administration, procurement, warehousing, production line worker (and many others), then it should be fine as lack of familiarity isn't such an issue.

Obviously, there are exceptions. Possibly a candidate for a management position may take too long to come to grips with a new industry and its issues, or they may lack the personal network that is often a component of success.

Personally, I've always championed a third option – a place where you can get the best of Options 1 and 2 (above), but with a whole lot more candidates than either location alone. It's a place where there are lots of candidates who Can do the job.

I refer to it as "The Periphery" – neither inside, nor outside.

A good way to think of this concept is to imagine the circles that spread out on an archery board.

You don't need to hit the bullseye. Anywhere on the board will do.

The dark bullseye is your company. Touching it is a larger white section, followed by another dark section, then another white and finally, one more dark. Notice how the circles get bigger as you move outwards (this means there are more choices for candidates as you move outwards). Now, imagine those other circles as being on the "periphery" of your company and the industry you operate in. Even the outermost red circle will still have several things in common with your industry.

Let's imagine your company installs cladding on the side of residential homes and you need a new operations manager (someone who will allocate materials and schedule the installation crews who do the work).

There's no doubt that an operations manager who works for a roof installation company could easily "**Do the job**" in a cladding company.

In the same way, a salesperson who has been selling doors for a home renovation company could easily work for a company that sells windows for new homes.

Sell one, sell any. A successful salesperson can easily move between these three building products.

All three industries sell products that are fixed to the outside of homes. The installations are mostly performed by carpenters, and all involve salespeople taking estimates of wall sizes and openings in the building. As we move towards the outer circles on our board, we can imagine that other relevant companies and industries might include brick sales, cement sales, internal wall linings, carpets etc. All are involved in residential homes.

There are a range of benefits to using this periphery approach, but let me just mention a few of the key ones:

1. Your candidates will be enthused about stepping away from one company and its industry and starting afresh in a similar but new industry.
2. The "ramp-up" (training) time for your new employee will be shorter, because of the similarities between the industries.
3. Your candidate (new employee) may bring new approaches, methods, or systems to your company – i.e., their previous company/industry may be more advanced than yours.
4. Similar to Point 3, your new employee might get to learn something new from your company, which should increase their job satisfaction and aid retention.

There may well be other benefits, but these few examples show how it can be a win-win for both sides when you consider candidates from the periphery of your industry.

And on that basis – you guessed it, **the sixth ingredient in the Secret Sauce is...**

Look to the periphery for great candidates

Chapter 9
Let me look into your soul
(The art of the interview)

Here's what you need to look out for. After this, it's our Interview Masterclass series

Chapter rating

A great drive. Lots of interesting scenery. Enjoy.

It's perhaps no surprise that this chapter is one of the largest in the book because arguably, no step in the hiring process is more important than interviewing. It's here where the person-to-person exchange takes place. It's also usually the first time we meet in person and our human emotions begin to play a role (on both sides). As much as a good interview can deliver to us, the potential exists for either side to make one or more mistakes. After conducting just over 800 interviews, it remains my favourite part of the hiring process. The good news is you only need to do a few interviews– using the right proforma. Your results can then be as good as mine – and that's a promise.

It could be argued that completing a professional interview provides you with up to 70% of the candidate "picture"

The remaining 30% is of course, still crucial, and you will be adding it in later, through the other Secret Sauce steps.

While the J.D is the main underpinning of Hiring's Secret Sauce, if you had to choose one step (and one step only) for a hiring exercise, it would have to be interviewing.

Here are the things that really matter when it comes to interviewing. Tried and proven – over 800 times.

Don't be afraid. It won't hurt a bit.

The art of interviewing has always been hampered by polite society – we don't want to offend, and we feel compelled to accept people on face value.

Interviewing has been made even more challenging by the various privacy laws that exist today, along with recent shifts in the way many people interact (with others). Some interpersonal boundaries are certainly real, while others are more self-imposed or even imagined.

While arguably more noticeable among millennials, it's obvious that a significant number of people today have become more awkward in one-to-one discussions, with many seemingly afraid they will cause offence in some way.

The challenge as an interviewer is to cut through these barriers to learn what you need to learn about your candidate. I say "learn" rather than for example, "collect information". That's because while information gathering is a key part of the interview, there is more you need to learn about the candidate which is above and beyond "information".

Interviewing is about building the candidate's story and a clear picture of them – a story which you note, evaluate, and thereafter confirm throughout the interview and subsequently, via psychometric testing, reference checking and where relevant, the sighting of supporting documentation. You then complete your picture of the candidate.

Because a variety of emotions can come into play for both the interviewer and the candidate, you need a method of negating these emotions and issues while remaining objective and collecting the vital information you require.

The very best method to achieve this is by using a professionally created interview proforma.

It provides you with the six things absolutely essential to a successful interview.

They are:

1. Focused questions which uncover the candidate's competencies and preferences across several workplace-related constructs.
2. Removal of any potential bias or prejudice by remaining completely neutral and objective.
3. A scoring system to measure, compare and rank all your interviewed candidates.
4. Works with, and directly feeds into, a corresponding reference check proforma.
5. Works with a preceding Telephone Screening proforma for reinforcement and repeatability.
6. Is designed by an Organizational Psychologist for validity.

Got the right time?

With an interview proforma in hand (let's assume the Secret Sauce proforma), you need to allocate one hour for your interview. Here's what to look out for:

- Forty to sixty minutes (40 – 60) represents the minimum to maximum time. Any tour of your facilities, including introductions to other staff, is additional to this timeframe.

- If more than one hour, then you are hopefully in the room with an outstanding candidate who is providing substantial and relevant answers to your questions. Alternatively, the opposite might be true – a candidate who is talking excessively (but is mostly off-topic or providing irrelevant information).

- Anything less than thirty minutes indicates a candidate of few words (or few achievements) who is unlikely to be providing the type of relevant and detailed responses you need. The exception is of course, junior positions or recent graduates who are without much notable work experience.

- Be cognisant of any candidate that tries to use up five, ten or even fifteen minutes in small talk, before the formal interview begins. Some candidates place excessive emphasis on rapport building, in the hope it might create an advantage for them, or often, that it might cover for any lack of quality answers on their part.

Welcome them like an old friend

In Chapter 8, I outlined some examples of bad body language. All you need to do is the opposite of those examples. I strongly recommend you place some effort into a positive and welcoming approach to your candidate(s) from the moment they walk in.

Well, perhaps not a hug, but you get the idea.

Spend a few minutes before the official start to engage in some small talk - ask about their journey to the interview, how their day has been going thus far etc. A few minutes is all you need. I've mentioned this before – a happy and relaxed candidate, is an open and receptive candidate. You will get a lot more out of the interview if you can achieve this.

This approach extends for every minute until the interview concludes – be friendly.

The title of this sub-heading is "It won't hurt a bit". In a nutshell, it's up to you as the interviewer to achieve that. Your task is to become their friend during the interview. Forget any notions of instilling a power imbalance or hierarchy. You don't need to do anything along those lines because any thinking candidate already knows a power imbalance is there.

Set the format (it helps)

By following a format (and communicating it to the candidate), you will further put them at ease, maximizing the benefits you will gain from the interview. Here's how I go about it:

- Begin by explaining you will be asking a series of 15 – 20 questions (even holding up your proforma).
- Explain that the proforma allows you to make accurate (and fair) comparisons between all candidates. Candidates seem to appreciate this statement.
- Explain that the interview will take anywhere up to one hour.
- Explain that while some time will be used up in writing down their answers, it's important that what they have to say is accurately recorded for later recollection.
- Advise them that there will be time allocated at the end of the interview to ask any questions they may have (and to please wait until then to ask).
- Advise them that at the end of the interview, you will outline the job role in detail (along with providing an overview of your company, its aims, products/services etc.) so that by the time they leave, they will have a clear understanding of what the job entails and in turn, whether they believe it will be a good fit for them. As a part of this, let them know that you have a job description which you will mutually review (while explaining that as an internal company document, they will unfortunately not be able to leave with a copy of it).
- Finally, explain that by leaving the job role discussion until the end, you will both have a feeling as to whether it's a good fit (or not).

Following this format keeps the interview on track and importantly, it enables you to (often) make a judgement about whether the candidate is right for your company and the job on offer. If not, then the mood is set for you to explain they will not be proceeding further in your hiring exercise.

Self-selecting (opting out).

You may find at the end of the interview (following a review of your J.D) that some candidates realise that either the job is not what they expected it to be, or that they do not believe they have the right skills (or desire) to do the job. There can be several reasons for this but the end result, is they opt out of your hiring exercise. While you might regret spending an hour with them, the truth is they have saved you from further headaches down the track. Once you've satisfied yourself that you explained your J.D fully and accurately, don't try and convince any candidate to stay the course and move further along your hiring process. It never works...

What the Secret Sauce interview method is really about

There's a core mantra that has underpinned my interviewing from day one.

Because it's so central to the Secret Sauce method, it follows me through the entire hiring process, although it really comes to the fore at the interview. You need to adopt it also.

It's the seventh ingredient of the Secret Sauce:

You need to always be thinking:

> **Can** they do the job, **will** they do the job *and,* **will** they fit in?

The various questions in the interview proforma work together to answer this mantra.

From the very beginning of an interview, and at every moment throughout, have this mantra front of mind. After logging your answer to each question and allocating its score, continue to view the candidate under this lens – in fact, continue this through psychometric testing, reference checking and, when discussing the offer of employment. Any doubt at any point, means further discovery or a rejection.

At the end of every interview, look carefully at the candidate while repeating this mantra in your mind. As usual, it should be reasonably clear if the answer is no, but in many instances, it could be a maybe, and you will need to move to psychometric testing and reference checking, to firm up your decision.

Let's break this mantra down a little:

Can they do the job? - Do they possess the right skills and work experience?

Will they do the job? – Are they motivated and driven to perform?

Will they fit in? – Will they fit your company culture?

Many/most of your candidates should meet the criteria of **Can they do the job?**

The content of their resumé along with your phone screening, should have uncovered a lot of what you need to know – although some of the questions which probe this first part of the mantra will only be asked during the interview. I'll leave it to your interview questioning to help you answer this key part of the mantra. The Secret Sauce Interview Proforma contains structured questions to answer this first part.

Secondly, and the more critical and harder to answer is **Will they do the job?**

"Will they" is all about Motivation and Drive. It can be viewed as the difference between intent and action although in some candidates (unfortunately), not even the intention to act will be clear enough.

This second part of the mantra is closely tied with the statement on the back cover of this book. It's about the 10% of people that make things happen.

"Will they do the job" is about demonstrating a track record of action and outcome. It's about the candidate performing enough of the activities (on a daily, weekly, and annual basis) to underpin those outcomes. Later in this book we will look at how two different candidates (one "making things happen" and the other not making things happen) are very easily contrasted. It's a great real-world example and an ideal way to learn so you get it right when interviewing.

Where's the value-add?

As you progress through the interview, you might begin to smile to yourself when you've found a candidate that can do the job and quite likely will do the job. Before we get to the last part of the mantra, there's another question to ask yourself before you move on.

It's a significant question and it's where the 10% of people that make things happen are truly found.

The question to ask yourself is: **Is that enough?**

In today's hyper-competitive economy, just doing the job may not be enough. In fact, you shouldn't accept it as being enough.

If you do, then you may find yourself dealing with the concept of mediocrity.

Mediocrity is a topic that features in the upcoming Interview Masterclass Series.

For now, it's all about the "**Value-add**".

Your candidate, (your future employee), needs to be a person that brings a tangible **value-add** to your business.

What is their special skill set or performance record that will bring the "something" your business requires, or has possibly lacked up until now?

What is that new skill or experience that will open up new opportunities, or deliver a new benefit to your business?

There needs to be something "extra" on offer. Something over and above the minimum.

How important is this to the Hiring Secret Sauce? – it's absolutely essential.

That's why it's the eighth ingredient in the Secret Sauce.

Search for the "value-add" in the candidates you interview.

Getting back to the mantra – **Will they fit in?**

Of the three questions in our mantra, this should be the easiest one for you to answer. It introduces us to the concept of "Company Culture".

You will find no shortage of views on how to define, measure or improve your company culture. A quick Google search on the term "company culture" yields over 11 billion results. You read that correctly: billion, not million. Surely, they can't be serious (with apologies to Flying High the movie).

I hate to bring reality to bear on such an emotive subject – a subject to which thousands of "consultants" try to earn their living by convincing you that your company culture needs immediate improvement (and their help), because without it, both you and your business are clearly headed for the corporate dustbin.

Now, if you've been in business for any amount of time and that business is at least moderately successful, then you already have a company culture – whether it's clearly defined or not. Of course, that's not to say that it might not need some improvement, but that's not in the scope of this book.

For the last twenty years, I've consistently heard the following when I have asked the manager - not so much how to define their company culture, but what a new employee needs to do, if they are to fit in, and thrive.

Overwhelmingly, the most common answer has been: *be productive, deliver results, and work well with our existing staff.* In the creativity-based companies I have worked with, the productivity requirement has sometimes been replaced by *demonstrating the required creative skills-abilities*, and more of an emphasis on interpersonal relationships with colleagues. I always felt that the creativity requirement was their version of being productive.

There is no doubt that companies with a younger average employee age, and those within the more dynamic or creative industries, are the more diverse and inclusive industries – and accordingly, strive to be more values-based. The software gaming industry is one that readily comes to mind.

When I canvass the views of employees as opposed to management, most point to work flexibility, skills development, scope for advancement, and opportunities to socialize or work within smaller teams where camaraderie is highest.

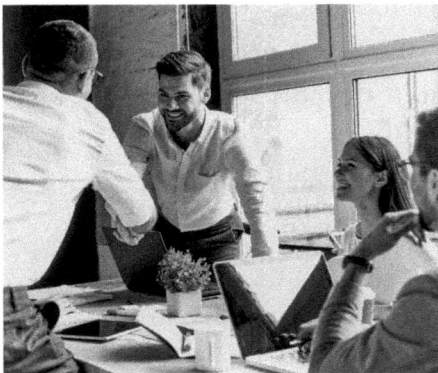

The culture of a given enterprise then, is at least to an equal extent, dictated by management – if not through formal policy, then through unspoken "expectations" and an inherent understanding by staff of which behaviors are encouraged, and which practices are discouraged.

Management is often focused on providing the most flexible arrangements that will still secure their required revenue, profitability, and market share. In other words, the financial realities of the business impact on, and shape, the company culture to some extent. This third part of the mantra (**Will they fit in?**) is about you the employer, understanding what your particular company culture is, and knowing whether the candidate will fit that culture or not.

If your company culture is not clearly defined for your business, then I recommend noting which of your employees are the most successful in your business and listing the traits they display. Then think about how you would explain the "style" and "feel" of your company to an outsider. Put those two things together, and you're a long way toward explaining your company culture.

Think – "the perfect employee or the perfect candidate for your business". What do they look like (or what would they look like?)[26]. Now, compare this candidate to that perfect employee. Do they match up? Will they fit in? You may not be 100% certain during the interview, but the other steps of the Secret Sauce method – especially reference checking, will help answer this question for you.

One thing I can confidently state is that if you neglect this important question and the candidate does not fit in, then the "glue" may not hold.

A final word here on "fitting in".

I continue to meet people in business who tell me that they just "know" if a candidate is right for the job and if they will fit in.

They call it "Gut Instinct".

It's an interesting subject and it could be of some value in answering this last part of the mantra. Let's explore it a little more closely, shall we?

---

26. *Recall that in your Job Description there is a section: Snapshot – The Ideal Candidate.*

Gut instinct – good for recognising danger, not so good for making hiring decisions

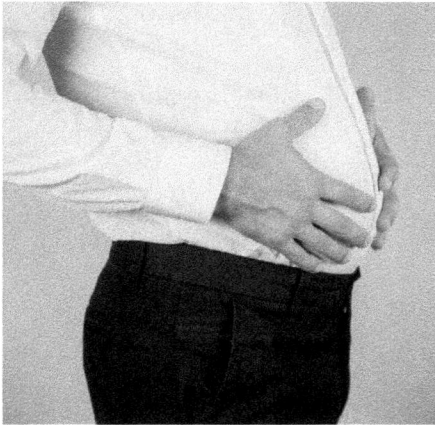

It's an obvious statement to make when we say people don't "think" with their stomach. You use your brain for that.

Anywhere on our bodies from the neck downward is involved in feeling.

So right up front, we're talking about feeling, not thinking.

Having said that, certain events that we experience can give us a bad (but important) feeling in our stomach.

If we experience an event in real time which has the potential to cause us great physical harm, then we can certainly get a nauseous feeling in our stomach.

So, our stomach or "gut" can confirm (and maybe allude), to impending danger, but it can't reason or compute logic for us. As an example, we can't use our gut instinct to tell us the difference between a small Toyota and a small Honda sitting next to each other in a car yard. We're going to need to look inside, read the brochures and ask questions to find that out. So, it's fair to say that gut instinct can't be relied on for a rational decision.

When we bring this back to the topic at hand – whether we can tell if a candidate will "fit" our company and its culture, well, we're back to that person-to-person interaction. Gut Instinct can tell us something here.

There's also the small matter of intuition (it's a real thing).

And while not always the case, it is more common to find a manager or employee who has worked with a significant number of people (usually over a lengthy period of time) to express a "feeling" about a certain candidate.

These feelings sometimes relate to knowledge of the type of employee that has been successful in let's say, the sales department of the company. The sales department might be full of gregarious types (Extroverts, – using the OCEAN model). While that's an obvious one, a more subtle example might be a candidate who is seeking to join your Admin team but has shown less of a focus on details during the interview.

Similar types?

And, where Owner-Managers are involved in the hiring process and the company is still small, there is sometimes a desire to hire very similar types to themselves (a winning formula in their mind!).

There is one more concept to discuss as part of this. It's what I refer to as "signals".

Signals are a component of body language and are also a part of intuition.

On some occasions, the cues that fall into the body language realm are so slight, so miniscule, that they're hard to express, let alone represent by using illustrations. Where this is the case, I refer to them as "signals".

An example of a signal is a slightly raised eyebrow, facial expressions that are very slight – perhaps a tendency to frown (or alternatively smile) at times when you think it's not appropriate. It can be a long and unwarranted stare at a colleague, a tendency to disregard one of the other interviewers in the room – a noticeable lack of respect shown to one of your colleagues.

All of these in my experience, are key drivers of a call of "gut instinct" by an employer/interviewer.

Gut instinct is, however, subject to many misinterpretations. On that basis I would recommend placing the final word on the answers you record on your interview proforma. You should value them ahead of any "feelings" during the interview.

A final word here on "signals" and your gut instinct in general. If there is at least one other person in your company that meets this particular candidate, be open and honest about your "feelings", and share them with that other person. Do they align?

If they do, then consider noting your feelings in the summary section of the Hiring Secret Sauce proforma, but you will need to confirm this via a second interview plus psychometric testing and reference checking.

Making a call of "gut instinct" is (sort of) OK during an interview, but you will need to convert it to logic at some point. If you can't convert it to logic, then you can't rely on it for your hiring decisions.

The Halo effect – the danger you won't see coming

While we're still in the realm of dealing with feelings, gut instinct and signals, there's another important person-to-person effect you need to be able to recognize – and deal with. It's known as the "Halo" effect.

At some point, you will find yourself interviewing a candidate that you just like.

If I were in that room with you and I asked you why you like this particular candidate, you might have some difficulty articulating what it is (about them) that you like.

But I won't – have any difficulty that is. I bet I know exactly what it is you like about them.

Let's start by assuming you're with a candidate that **can do the job.** Heck, let's even assume you believe they **will do the job.**

But it's not just these two things. There's something more. You're hitting it off like best buddies/BFF's.

I'll tell you what it is – the Halo effect is in play.

The Halo effect means you think they have a halo sitting on their heads - you think they're an angel. Well, they may or may not be an angel, but more than likely, they're of a similar age to you (they may even be the exact same age). At the very minimum, you're of the same demographic and likely the same cultural background. As the interview proceeds, you notice you have the same/similar view on a range of subjects.

A key tell-tale sign is that you both drift off-subject, talking about things you mutually have knowledge of. Your skills and experience are similar. Perhaps you're both working in the same industry – so you start discussing industry issues. A topic might spill into current events where you find you both have the same opinion. Or it might be hobbies – you both like the same kind of music – or sports.

What has happened here, is you've found a candidate who is – in many ways – just like you. You're two peas in a pod. You've got shared values, shared experiences, and common views on a range of topics.

In truth, the Halo effect is not about them being an angel – it's about your view of them. Your opinion of them has just been elevated because: they're just like you!

The Halo effect – they're just like you, and what's not to like about that?

The real danger here is that you may unconsciously award them higher scores on individual answers because you (possibly) regard yourself as the ideal employee, and here you have someone who is once again, *just like you.*

Your best approach here is to remain impartial and just focus on the score you allocate to each of the questions on your interview proforma. Don't deviate. Be impartial.

If you have the opportunity for a second interview, you should do so, while ensuring a colleague joins in.

Charisma, class, and character (a different kind of halo)

This book deliberately eschews using data, graphs etc. to support its views and that includes the citing of references - but in this instance, I am asking you to consider a few propositions that you may not agree with (or believe). On that basis, you may want to hit up Google to satisfy yourself. Here we go...

For hundreds (if not thousands) of years, charismatic people have obtained advantages for themselves in every aspect of life. Whether that's in love, war, or matters of money, it's a reality that few would deny. Good looking and charismatic people sell us products every day on our smartphones, TV's and in magazines.

As recently as the 1960's and 70's, experiments were performed of mock legal trials where it was found that individual jurors (not all of them) ascribed guilt to the less good-looking defendants, and regularly gave verdicts of not guilty to the good-looking defendants (or reduced the severity of their punishments). In summary, good-looking, charismatic defendants, got away with a lot more than their less good-looking counterparts.

Now, who isn't aware of an infamous person or two, that perhaps broke the law (or was very unscrupulous), but still managed to extract significant financial advantage for themselves - before being brought to heel. Again, it's very likely that charisma played a part.

There is one variable however when it comes to charisma. A variable that decides what degree of "advantage" the charismatic person will enjoy (if any at all) – and that variable is you. I'll explain more in a moment.

Occasionally (but not always), charisma travels with a companion. That companion is class. By class I don't mean inherent style and good taste – I'm referring to a perceived class advantage through either real or implied wealth.

This perceived class can bestow certain advantages. It might take the form of an education in a more reputable school or university. Alternatively, it may allow for a better street address and almost certainly better clothes, a better car, and perhaps even access to exclusive clubs. So, whether it's charisma or an upper-class candidate you find yourself with, you should be aware of how this might affect your hiring exercise.

Charisma, class, or perhaps both. But are they more credible as a result?

Class has been a frequent companion in my twenty plus years of recruitment experience.

Throughout those twenty years, I have treated every candidate in exactly the same manner. That is, by focusing only on the substance of the candidate, and never their style (or appearance).

Perceived class is just as often an issue for those individuals who regard themselves as upper class, as it is for anyone else.

Let me share an example of a candidate seeking a position in a major political party only a few short years ago.

This individual had been regarded as a solid *Party man*[27] in one particular State of the country, due to his history of successful fundraising for that party.

He now sought an important position within that same political party, but in one of the larger, more populous States. He was successful in that bid.

Later, when it was found that he had been defrauding said political party and profiting illegally, he was duly removed. An internal review was conducted, to understand what had gone wrong.

27. A "Party Man" is not to be confused with a "Party Boy" – a person who enjoys excessive drinking, dancing etc.

When the review was relayed to me by a contact inside that political party, the discussion went along these lines:

"Don't tell me - let me guess. This individual had been a successful fundraiser for the Party, was a member of all the "right" social clubs and was generally regarded as a "Good Fellow". As a result, you (The political party) gave him an undue amount of latitude, and did not put him through a thorough hiring process"?

"Exactly", came the response.

The individual in question certainly had a degree of charisma about him.

So, charisma and *perceived* class can be forms of a halo which may sway you – perhaps not consciously. Your method for dealing with it? – disregard their appearance and posture completely. If they live in an upmarket neighborhood or dress expensively, completely disregard it and focus on what they do, and how they go about it. Using your interview proforma, apply all the Secret Sauce ingredients. Put them under a microscope and perhaps even scrutinize them to a higher degree than normal – given that their charisma may well be accompanied by above average verbal communication skills. Don't let a charismatic candidate enjoy any form of advantage. It's entirely up to you!

We're done now with gut instinct, the halo effect and charisma (all the little things that can cloud our judgement). It's now time to look at something you can rely on.

Past (work) performance is an indicator of future performance

If you've ever viewed an advertisement for a financial product or service, you'll notice they all have the same disclaimer - *Past performance is not an indicator of future performance.*

I've always found that amusing because in the world of hiring, it's the exact opposite.

By now, I think you know why it would be the case.

It's because either nature or nurture has established our personality traits for us, and, as we saw in the OCEAN personality model, our traits drive our actions both at work, and in our personal lives.

In fact, I'd say that past performance **is the best indicator of future performance**.

As we get closer to The Interview Room, it pays to keep this mantra in mind. It belongs right up there with **Can they do the job, will they do the job,** *and* **will they fit in?**

If you've got an action-oriented, results-focused candidate in front of you, I'll wager in the previous jobs they have held, that there is a quantifiable pattern of workplace achievement. If you've got a details-focused, highly conscientious candidate, then I'll also wager those traits were evidenced in their past work history.

If you can establish a certain pattern of behavior during your interview (by examining their resumé/work history and, if you can corroborate this via psychometric testing and reference checking), then you can be reasonably certain they will approach your job vacancy in the same way. Understand the candidate's work history, and you can predict more of the same if they join your company. Obviously, factors around specific job motivation and company fit, need to be satisfied also. That is to say, providing your job fits with their aspirations and your "company culture" is a fit, then you can be quite confident.

Candidates with a track record of productivity should still be productive next month – unless something goes wrong.

As a spoiler, there are circumstances where this mantra won't hold true.

From experience, this tends to occur where the career aspirations (or more commonly), the personal life goals of the candidate, diverge or are changing.

In these instances, you may find a candidate who has performed at an operative level and has simply outgrown the role, or is about to. For example, let's assume they are an IT technician. You might hire them based on their exceptional eight (8) years of high-level performance but in their mind, it's well past the time when they should have been promoted to a Project Management role. As their enthusiasm wanes, their performance drops away a little.

Another example could be an Analyst who has worked in the Stock Market for many years. Along the way they've been building up their own personal share portfolio. It's now doing very nicely thank you. Their traditional 10 hour per day working week now starts to look less appealing than it once did.

But all things being equal, this mantra holds true. And that means – you guessed it, **it's the ninth ingredient in the Secret Sauce:**

> **SECRET HIRING'S SAUCE** | **Past performance is the best indicator of future performance.**

Making a shortlist (Hint: it's got nothing to do with height)

You might think that the point of interviewing is to find your preferred candidate (*The One*). While that is your ultimate goal, your real aim at this stage is to identify a small group of preferred candidates (known as a shortlist). Somewhere between two and four candidates is about right. Certainly not less than two, but perhaps as many as six.

You need to be working with a small handful because you still have three crucial steps to go after interviewing – namely psychometric testing, reference checking, and the offer stage (employment contract).

Things can (and occasionally do) go wrong during those stages (although the risks drop away proportionately as you move through the individual steps). The main point to take away is that you need to have a shortlist following your interviewing. If you don't have at least two or three solid prospects, then keep advertising.

And very importantly, keep your entire shortlist "warm" until your preferred candidate has signed your employment contract. This means regular contact to let them know they are all still in contention.

So, now that we know the what and the who, it's time for us to look at the how.

Time to step into The Interview Room...

Chapter 10
Interview Masterclass Series
(Levelling up!)

This is where you move from novice to professional.

Chapter rating

After this, you really ARE a professional.

Welcome to the Masterclass series.

As we enter the interview room, there are two items you need. The first is a proforma that works for every job role, and the second are some high-end interviewing techniques which supplement the questions on the proforma – and that's what this Masterclass series is all about.

Interview Questions

Interview Questions
Date:

Position applied for:

Applicant/Candidate Name:

Contact phone number:

Contact email address:

Street address:

Education and Qualifications
Highest formal qualifications obtained:

The proforma includes several ways in which you can ask each particular question. This has been done because some candidates will hear a question slightly differently from others. While the interview proforma is all you need, this Masterclass series is about teaching you my personal interviewing techniques. It's the way in which I get the ultimate cut-through. It works - and it works extremely well. Put the two together and, well, now you're levelling up…

Expansion questioning (Interview Masterclass, No 1).

We're beginning the Masterclass series by looking at a candidate who is lying about an achievement – because it's *the* ideal way to impart a technique which will become a cornerstone of your interviewing. To avoid using industry specific jargon, we'll use a sales example from Chapter 7:

Dirty Dozen No 6 – *Did not achieve the claims they make for themselves (i.e., increased sales by 70% each year for four years).*

For our purposes, let's assume this candidate sold electric drills (power tools). Expansion questioning works like this...

So, tell me exactly how you went about it?

You can think of expansion questioning as trying to uncover what parts go in to making an electric drill. The technique is about breaking down the claimed achievement into smaller pieces for examination. Only then can we know if the candidate had all the necessary parts to make that drill (i.e.: achieve the success they claimed).

To begin, I would ask who the clients were for the electric drills –
i.e.: were they sold to hardware stores, construction companies, or direct
to tradespeople via a website?

It's a very simple question – "Who were your clients"?

If hardware stores were part of the answer, I'd then ask for the names
of those hardware stores. I'd do the same for the construction
companies.

Whether the candidate answers "all, or some combination of the
above", I would immediately ask for the percentage breakdown – let's
assume they respond with 60% of sales were to hardware stores, 25% to
construction companies, and the remaining 15% via online sales.

If they respond with anything along the lines of *"I'm not sure of the
breakdown because we had admin staff that kept the figures"*, well then, I'm
already skeptical because anyone who is claiming 70% annual sales
growth, certainly knows how they went about it.

Assuming you got an acceptable answer then…

Next (expansion) question: "In year 1, what was the sales revenue
(starting point) for this incredible four-year run of success?"

Again, I'm expecting a *very* clear answer on this. Let's assume the
candidate advises it was $400,000.

In the background, I can calculate that after the first year, the revenue would be $680,000, year two it rises to $1,156,000, year three $1,965,200 and year four $3,340,840

So, after four years of compounding 70% growth, we have an eight-fold increase in revenue (from $400K to $3.3 Million). If you're after a salesperson, then you need to make sure *this* candidate doesn't leave the interview room without signing your employment contract. In fact, just forget about the remainder of the Secret Sauce method...

In reality, alarm bells should now be starting to ring in your ears.

Let's continue the expansion questioning:

"Did you achieve this performance on your own, or were there other staff involved?"

If the candidate claims it was all down to them, then my skepticism goes up another notch - however they do need to be given the opportunity to prove their claim.

Now, we can be reasonably certain the candidate isn't the only one involved in selling $3.3 million worth of power tools each year[28] – and I'm not just referring to the order processing and dispatch staff who would be involved in moving that much product.

As we continue to explore this claimed achievement, it's also a fair assumption that the 15% of sales via their online portal were handled

28. *This specific question - who else was involved, or who else supported the candidate, would become an extra (custom) question to include in your reference checking. Assuming this candidate progresses that far.*

by one or more other staff. Why is that? – simply because they're completely different job functions. Would anybody really expect the salesperson who is on the road visiting the construction companies and hardware stores, to be simultaneously managing the on-line portal? On this small but important point, I would outline this view to the candidate, and see whether we can attribute the 15% (or a good part of it) to one or more other staff.

To continue, the interview proforma uncovers whether they have been performing the activities necessary to support this level of sales performance.

The next question to ask is whether the candidate grew the business by:

A. Identifying new customers (construction companies and hardware stores they weren't previously selling to) – i.e., more users or:

B. Whether it was by selling more tools to the same construction companies and hardware stores – i.e., more usage.

Let's assume the answer was A - bringing new customers on board because to be honest, the new client path/more users is the only realistic way the claimed 70% sales growth could occur. If their answer is

B., then not only is it highly unlikely, but there's now a fair chance the candidate is more of an account manager, rather than a sales executive/ business developer, who prospects and wins new clients (new business).

Incidentally, what does your job description and advert say? Is it a new business developer you're after or an account manager?

As an aside (and to be blunt), account managers are generally not as proactive as salespeople. They still have good interpersonal skills, but they tend not to be the high activity, always on the telephone, always on the road salespeople, that win new business.

At this point (actually, right from the beginning), there were only ever four possibilities:

1. There were other staff involved in achieving the 70% growth rate.
2. The 70% annual growth rate was more like 10-20%.
3. The starting point in year 1 was significantly lower –i.e.: $100,000 not $400,000.
4. Some combination of the above.

And here we have the tenth ingredient of the Secret Sauce –

Deconstruct. Dig deeper. Demand details.

It's a near certainty this candidate is lying but if it's point number 1, then it's the perfect segue into our next Masterclass example. (Of course, our example here is based on a fictitious candidate and a manufactured lie, but please continue to play along as I try to impart these advanced interviewing techniques).

We versus I (Interview Masterclass No 2)

We versus I is a central theme in Hiring's Secret Sauce. In fact, knowing how to separate the "We" from the "I", is crucial to interview success.

"We versus I" isn't strictly a lie. It's not exactly embellishment, nor is it clearly obfuscation. It's a combination of all three.

During an interview, it's a candidate's use of the plural terms "we" or "us" versus the singular "I" that is the issue.

Of course, "we" or "us" can speak to teamwork – an important attribute in every employee however, when it comes to discussing achievements or the duties and responsibilities performed by the candidate, then we need to separate out the "I" – to understand the part they alone played.

You can think of it in these terms: you are hiring one person, not a group of people. You therefore need to know what *this particular candidate* delivered, what *they* achieved, how *they* went about performing their role. It's a time when you need to uncover what their (and no-one else's) contribution was.

Let's get back to our power tools candidate for reference:

How did you achieve such an impressive growth rate of 70% compounding per annum?

*Well, **we** worked extremely hard and got the result or:*

***We** made a lot of sales calls to win new business or:*

***We** put together some great advertising campaigns, which helped **us** get the result.*

A candidate using the "we" or "us" term is really giving you a clear view of their subconscious. They're telling you it was a collaborative effort.

At this point you need to ask a direct question. I would typically frame it as follows:

*You've talked about "we" achieving this level of sales. When you say "we", who were the other staff involved, and what roles did they have? I'd like to understand exactly who the "we" are, and what they did. What was your exact part in this? What specifically were the activities **you** undertook, that were separate from the other staff involved, and how did these activities deliver that level of sales?*

Alternatively:

It sounds like you were one of several staff involved in achieving these results. Can you please clarify exactly what functions you performed, and who were the other staff alongside you? For those other staff members, please outline what duties they performed.

This is the eleventh ingredient in the Secret Sauce:

> **"We" is where the pretenders hide, "I" is the achiever.**

Look for the "I" and don't accept the "We" or "Us".

Believable achievements (Interview Masterclass, No 3)

The opposite of our previous example is the high performing candidate that delivers all the things we want in a great employee. So, let me introduce Daniel to you.

The all-time top scorer.

The Secret Sauce Interview form contains four categories each with a 1 to 5 scoring range. In twenty years, Daniel is the only candidate to have scored 5 for each category.

Daniel was a Project Manager. Rather than repeat the expansion questioning of our earlier sales example - **Deconstruct. Dig deeper. Demand details**, let's trust that the way in which Daniel managed and delivered projects, was consistent with a results–oriented, high achiever. I'm sure you understand your own industry well enough to be able to do the same with your candidates.

Naturally enough, he was hired and performed brilliantly as a Project Manager before rising to become a General Manager. So, what made Daniel such a great candidate?

Let's review his interview proforma and consider his overall interview performance:

- His skills and experience were directly relevant to the employer and their industry.
- Daniel provided relevant details for each question – without prompting.
- When asked for greater detail, he provided additional relevant information – demonstrating significant lived experience.
- At the same time, his answers were concise, with no unnecessary elaboration.
- Daniel stayed on topic, answering only the question at hand - where many others drift off to other areas.
- He remained patient throughout, waiting for each successive question to be asked before talking.
- The additional detail sought about one of Daniel's achievements was freely provided.
- The fine details of the project demonstrated a significant "value-add" to his previous employer. His advanced project management skills align perfectly with the future growth plans of his prospective employer.
- Impressions of a proactive, conscientious, people-oriented employee, were subsequently confirmed via psychometric testing and reference checking.
- All of Daniel's claimed achievements were verified by his referees.

Of course, many other traits and characteristics go into making a great candidate, and we've explored those in previous chapters.

However, for now, there's another obvious candidate type we should review. One which helps to further contrast the good candidates from the others.

It's the candidate who technically does nothing wrong but is perhaps mediocre. They fail to inspire and most notably, there's no identifiable value-add.

I just happen to have one right here...

Indifferent, low-impact candidates (Interview Masterclass No 4)

I'd like to introduce another secret sauce ingredient right here. **It's the twelfth Secret Sauce ingredient:**

> **Mediocrity is death.**

Sounds a little harsh I know, but the reality is that companies who hire average candidates die a slow death. I've witnessed it many times. Those companies who hire good / great candidates are always successful and often outperform their competitors. Those who hire mediocre candidates tend to hang on for a while (longer if they have a good product or service), but ultimately fall behind and drop away.

The trap is often a burning desire to hire quickly – to fill a vacancy so you can move on to other priorities. In these instances, there's a tendency to accept candidates who are "good enough". Don't do it! Be prepared to repeat your hiring exercise, if necessary, rather than accept mediocrity.

As an example, let's consider John. He was interviewed for a management role in a company that was growing strongly. As we can see, John's interview was brief. A review of his interview proforma shows how this occurred.

- John's skills were only broadly in-line with the employer's requirements, rather than being a strong fit.
- Answers provided were non-expansive (just the minimum was offered).
- His answers were unimpressive, resulting in brief note taking.
- John's cited achievements provided no real value-add to the employer.
- John's claimed achievements were only the normal duties expected of a manager.
- He cited money as a key motivator.
- John was focused on spending more time on his recently acquired rural property (showed signs of an indifference to work / building a career).
- Low-to-average scores on the 1 to 5 scale support a poor overall rating.

Where Daniel was striving forward to his next achievement, John was looking to enjoy life more – one in career building mode, the other in lifestyle mode.

It shouldn't be this hard.

There are a few other obvious signs that you're sitting down with a low–impact candidate.

Top of the list has always been a boring conversation headed by a lack of interpersonal connection. You just feel like it's going to be a slow, uninspiring interview. You're trying to connect with this person but they're not responding to your attempts to build some rapport. You get the impression they would rather be somewhere else.

Second on the list are brief answers to your questions. You've asked a serious question, but you're struggling to get more than a few words written on your interview proforma. With some of these candidates, you stay on the same question, asking for more detail. Often, this type of candidate just can't give you more.

Third is an inability to answer the actual question. At worst, they don't understand the meaning of the question and give you a substantially different answer. In their mind, they've heard something different to what you asked.

And last but not least, a tendency to run past their answer and drift into areas you didn't ask about. Often, once they've answered the specific question, I'll interject to keep the interview on track.

Ultimately it all feels like this:

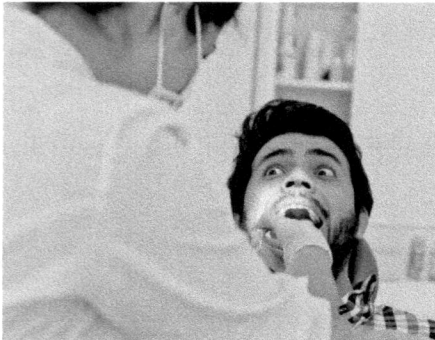

The entire exercise is as difficult and as uncomfortable as pulling teeth. It shouldn't be that way, but when you encounter it with a candidate, well, you certainly know it.

The fifth and final act in our Masterclass series follows over the page.

It was, in reality, another "Tale from The Vault" but I decided it provided a great way to end the Masterclass series. I hope you agree:

Danger, Will Robinson, danger! (Interview Masterclass No 5)
(With apologies to Irwin Allen/Lost in Space).

Background

Is it possible for a candidate to get around the Hiring Secret Sauce method?

This book provides the method, and our various proforma documents are the tools. Combine the two, and you should be able to accurately assess any candidate – be they great, average or below-average. That's the promise.

Our protagonist here was quite possibly the closest a candidate came to breaking through. In my defense, they didn't get past me…well, did they kind of? - I don't want to spoil it. Read on and judge for yourself.

It's going to be a very tough day...

Alarm bells begin to sound in my head (softly at first) as Michelle enters the interview room.

Within ten minutes those alarm bells get a lot louder, as I realize that I have three distinct issues on my hands - issues that are going to require some real skill to manage. Issues that could easily bring this hiring exercise undone...

You see, Michelle "**Can do the job**" (the right skills are there) but I have my doubts over whether she "**Will do the job**" and just as importantly if she will "**Fit in**".

My first issue is that Michelle has only ever worked in academia. Immediately following her undergraduate degree, she completed a master's degree in accounting and finance, and then stayed on as a lecturer at the University. The reasons she is giving me for wanting to step out of academia and into industry, aren't very convincing.

I'm concerned that if she doesn't like what she finds in this job (working as a management accountant), that she can just pick up the phone to her professor and be back at the university within the week. I need to explore this a bit more (and reference checking is the best tool for this) – more on that later.

My second issue is that Michelle is very obviously keeping her cards close to her chest. She is only giving me the bare minimum of information essential to the questions at hand. I can't get Michelle to expand and give me more. I'm constantly left feeling that she is trying to manage the information gathering process. I certainly let Michelle know that I know what she is doing[29].

Michelle is clearly intelligent – she's also perceptive enough to realize that I am not totally convinced or happy with how the interview is unfolding. But Michelle also knows that she is a strong prospect for this job – strong enough to get her onto the shortlist and to be interviewed by my client (the Finance Manager at ABC Industrial Group).

Michelle also knows that if she is interviewed by the employer, that she will have a distinct advantage over the other candidates. And I know she is absolutely correct about that.

This last point is to do with issue number three, and it's the one I'm most concerned about.

You see, Michelle is very obviously the long-lost twin sister of a beautiful, and well-known, actress of South African descent.

Tall, lithe, and stunningly beautiful, Michelle contrasts perfectly with my client at ABC Industrial Co LLC – a middle-aged not especially handsome man who I suspect will be unable to withstand Michelle's charms.

My strategy to avert this looming disaster? I make sure that one of my three reference checks is with her university professor, and I put one of my standard questions to him: If Michelle's "experiment" with working in industry isn't to her liking, and she calls you to get her old job back, would you take her back?" "Yes" came the very honest reply.

---

29. *This is a warning sign you should keep in mind. Refusing to elaborate/expand, is not acceptable.*

This is shared with my client (the Finance Manager), packaged up with reasons why candidate's 1 and 2 are equally strong prospects for this job role, but with no risks attached.

Just a stock photo and, if you think there's a resemblance to a famous actress, well that's on you.

The outcome? Movie star looks win. Michelle is hired. Four months later her experiment with industry is over. She resigns and returns to her old job at the university. The client freely acknowledges that he acted against my advice, and so would not be asking me to re-fill the vacancy under our guarantee arrangement. He would "sit" on things for a few months while he re-thought the need for that position in the company. He clearly felt some personal responsibility and needed time to process what had happened.

Now, in the 21st century, some readers might be asking themselves if this could really be an issue. Surely, the manager at ABC Industrial would be professional enough to not allow good looks to become an issue. All I can tell you is (just like every other anecdote in this book), that is how it actually went down. And to further my defense, recall earlier in Chapter 9 about the ability of the charismatic to influence us.

But, admittedly, this was an unusual case.

Michelle is perhaps *the* example of where charisma, good looks, *perceived* class and strong qualifications, combined into a very effective and difficult-to-resist individual.

The fact remains however that she was wrong for the job role. Following the Secret Sauce method with the proforma's gave all the required warnings to avert this disaster in waiting.

And that's the simple message here in this, our final example in the Masterclass series.

What's next? At the beginning of this fifth and final example in our Masterclass series, I said it could have easily been placed in our Tales from The Vault series, but the movie star's twin carried through to the employer, and involved reference checking. There was just too much going on. This next story, however, just had to be in the Tales from The Vault series. The poor guy. It still seems like yesterday when he walked into our office...

TALES FROM THE V🔒ULT

First impressions count - but not always!

Seth has just arrived for his interview. He's clearly nervous and looking very uncomfortable. I suspect he was running late and needed to break into a sprint to make it on time. I also notice he is wearing a heavy suit which probably isn't helping on this warm summer day.

To make Seth feel more comfortable, I stand up and remove my jacket inviting him to do the same. I explain that the building's air conditioning system isn't very good, and it often gets quite warm in this room (not true). He doesn't follow my lead, which I thought was unusual, although the reason for that soon became clear.

With Seth's face a bright shade of red before I even ask my first question - and sweat beading furiously on his brow, I make an excuse to leave the room (I wanted to give him some time to compose himself). I returned three minutes later with a small folder as a prop (which I didn't really need). Seth looked slightly more composed.

Back in Chapter 8, I outlined an ingredient which was to **"Always make your candidate comfortable"**. In this way, you tend to get more from them. In keeping with that theme, I ease into the questioning and try to lighten the mood with some small talk – but regardless of what I try, there seems little I can do to make Seth relax and, well, my own mind is now beginning to wander…

As Seth is still bright red and still sweating (Sweaty Seth, I have anointed him) my mind is turning to the relative merits of polyester versus cotton when it comes to making men's shirts. I'm sitting here trying to recall the properties of both materials. My recollection is that cotton allows the skin to breathe, while polyester holds its shape better.

I think it's likely that Seth is wearing a blended shirt – a mixture of both materials. I think to myself: *There must be an upper limit to the amount of sweat cotton can*

absorb? (and I think we're almost there)! At only one-third of the way through the interview, Seth's shirt is now clinging to him like wet toilet paper. As his face has been bright red since we first sat down – and has not settled at all, I'm starting to wonder if I actually need to be concerned about his health. Might this be the first interview I've ever conducted where I need to call a medical time-out?

For the first time ever, I change the format of the interview. I start to talk about current economic issues – given we're here for an economist's role in an investment bank. I ask Seth for his views, then I ask him which football team he supports. I decide we should break for a coffee, and I continue my questioning as we watch the bustling city life outside the office window. I consign all his answers to memory – I've stopped writing things down in front of him (I suspect it was contributing to his anxiety). Even by my own standards of hospitality, I've gone above and beyond. But why have I done this?

Simple really. Seth's answers to my first few questions (combined with his resumé and our phone screening), were telling me that he fits the Job Description perfectly. I also knew his personality (once he overcame his nervousness), was going to fit in nicely with the existing team. So, I knew Seth **Could do the job**, and I knew he would definitely **Fit in**. Of course, we still had to answer whether he **Would do the job**, but as you probably know by now, answering that part of the mantra is best served by psychometric testing and reference checking. The relevant questions in our interview proforma certainly go some of the way to answering that, and as we also now know; **Past performance is the best indicator of future performance.** Seth's work history is checking out and holding up against the questions on my interview proforma.

As we're getting towards the end of our content on Interviewing, I'm hoping that the combined ingredients of the Secret Sauce are starting to come together for you. Seth was a great example of looking past (or through) some challenges during the interview because you knew that you were applying many (or most) of the Secret Sauce ingredients, and he was coming through shining (and not just shining from the sweat on his brow…).

And, we haven't heard the last of Seth. He makes another appearance later in the book.

Chapter 11
Interviews
(The sequel)

To be continued...

Chapter rating

Easy. Just keep your hands on the wheel.

There was a little bit of a risk in calling this chapter "The sequel" because if the word "sequel" conjures up images of a movie theater to you , and your history of watching movies is anything like mine, then the sequel is rarely as good as the original.

Of course, there are different types of sequels (or acts that come afterwards). For example, there is the encore after a great music concert. It looks like it's all over, the stage has gone black, the performers have walked off but all-of-a-sudden, they're back for more!

The encore is that little bit extra you just *have to have* before you can walk away truly satisfied, and the same thing can be said after the first round of interviews with your shortlisted candidates. While the preferred candidate often crystallizes after that first interview, it's sometimes not until a second interview that they truly lock in – or on occasion, fall over (and you need to progress another shortlisted candidate). So, what we're talking about here is a sequel – one you need to go through in order for your interview stage to be truly complete. For all those reasons and more, here's how that encore performance may need to go for you.

Second interviews (do we really love each other?)

Converting a candidate into an employee is a long-term serious commitment (at least, that's what you're hoping for). It goes without saying that you want to be as certain as you can. With that in mind, one of the things that has shown itself to be of enormous value (and which doesn't really use up much of your time), is a second interview.

In my experience, skipping a second interview can be a cause of losing your preferred candidate - because you lost an opportunity to stay connected and continue building your knowledge and comfort level with each other.

A second interview often delivers greater insight – which might help you avoid a hiring mistake. And of course, assuming it all goes right, it can reconfirm your preferred candidate – giving you the extra confidence to proceed.

While it's a short topic, it's no less important.

Here's why second interviews should be part of your hiring process:

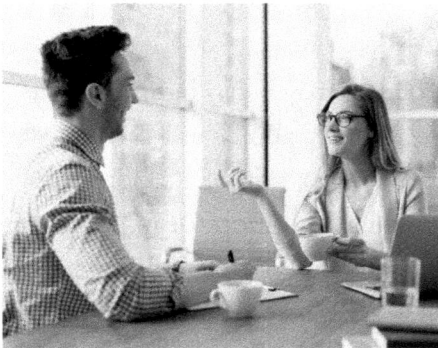

- Second-round interviews tend to be more relaxed for both parties and as a result, are usually more productive. You will *almost certainly* learn something new.
- Second-round interviews either re-confirm your preferred candidate, or help you separate one or more candidates from your first-round interviews.

- A second-round interview is a great opportunity to delve more deeply into the candidate's competencies - by having them expand on earlier answers, or by providing new examples (the nervousness of first-round interviews sometimes causes them to forget).
- A second interview is the ideal time to apply a job specific test – see below.
- You can ask more situational questions – i.e.: how the candidate sees the position unfolding, and how they see themselves contributing to your company (since they would have gained an understanding of your company from the first interview).

What to look out for... (The good).
- Look for candidates who have conducted their own research into your company during the intervening period. The candidate should now be able to guess at some of the trends or issues that might be impacting on your company, and your industry in general. Remember, interest *is* enthusiasm.

What to look out for... (The bad).
- Excessive questioning by the candidate may be an indication they are comparing job opportunities, and may also be at a second-round interview elsewhere. It can also be a sign of a candidate that is not yet ready to commit to a new position (or in particular, to join your company). If they have not already been forthright about any other opportunities they are pursuing, use this time to clarify their situation.
- Be wary of candidates who have not used the intervening period effectively – such as conducting more research into your company. It's often a sign they have other opportunities they are pursuing, are less interested in the position you are offering or, they feel they have the position "in the bag". Any of these reasons are areas for concern.

A major trap for employers at this second interview stage, is moving forward with a candidate that clearly **Can do the job**, but who is not demonstrating enough enthusiasm for the position — it's not certain they **Will do the job.** You need to be on the continual lookout for the necessary drive and enthusiasm essential in a good employee — but remember, your preferred candidate(s), should be progressing to psychometric testing to uncover their actual levels of motivation and drive.

If you haven't already done so, it's important to introduce the preferred candidate(s) to one or more of the staff in your company (if they exist) and take them for a detailed tour of your operation. A common reason heard from candidates as to why they selected one job opportunity over another, is the extra sense of confidence and comfort they gained by being given access to other staff, and viewing their future place of employment.

Now is the right time for a test

Second interviews are a great time to consider a job-specific test. With formalities largely taken care of during the first interview, candidates are now more receptive to tests. While full workplace simulations can be applied, they are an exercise in themselves to construct and deliver. Some smaller, easier to apply tests I have personally used include:

- Workbench tests for technicians (Are they truly familiar with the equipment they claim to be on their resumé?).
- Word or Excel tests for Admin staff.
- Financial analysis exercises for Fund Managers, Financial Planners etc.
- Simulated negotiations and meetings for Salespeople, Business Managers, Consultants etc.

Properly constructed and delivered during a second interview, a test or simulation can provide clarity (or concern) for employers. I highly recommend structuring at least a basic exercise at your second interview.

And the final reason why second interviews are so valuable? – they keep your preferred candidate(s) "warm" by keeping them connected to you.

As we already know from Chapter 4, talent doesn't wait around.

If you need to reject a candidate after a second interview.

It's worth repeating (Chapter 5) that any candidate you have met in person and is subsequently unsuccessful, should only ever receive a verbal rejection from you, and never any type of written communication – it's a recognition of their achievement in having got this far and of course, they might be ideal for a new job role you have somewhere down the track. It's in your interest to maintain a good relationship with them.

On our website you will find a separate document to cover the subject of verbal rejections, and it includes some typical phone scripts that you can use. Please refer to this document for further advice.

www.hiringsecretsauce.com

Panel interviews

Hiring's equivalent of a parole board hearing?

This panel interview subject has been placed next to our advice on second interviews and that's because it's often the format chosen if there is to be a second interview.

I generally advise against making the first interview a panel interview unless you've got no choice. The reason is that some candidates find them intimidating.

If like me, you subscribe to that view, then leave the panel format to your second interview. As the ice has already been broken during the first interview, some familiarity has been established, and that helps make a panel interview a little more comfortable. The candidate at least then knows one person on the panel.

Your top priority is to make sure your candidate never feels this way during a panel interview.

Panel interviews are one of the rare steps in the hiring process that can cause as many problems as benefits – if you're not careful.

There are two main reasons for this. The first is a poorly thought-out structure or objective, and the second is the overpowering/over-whelming effect. Fortunately, both are easily avoided.

So, who gets a seat on the panel?

The golden rule here is that if you do not have any direct involvement with the candidate, or you're not a stakeholder in their success or failure, then don't attend the panel interview.

I also recommend that panel interviews generally be reserved for management roles (supervisory level and above) and less so, for job roles at the operative level.

By operative level, I mean any job where the candidate has no direct reports of their own, and where they perform duties of a non-managerial nature.

In a role where that operative will need to work with a core group of employees (at their same level), they should ideally meet at least one of those employees following a successful interview - and arguably, one of those peers could certainly be on the panel. So, this may be the exception where you could apply a panel format for an operative level candidate. The inclusion of a peer can benefit the candidate as much as your company. Most candidates gain an extra level of comfort from talking to (or hearing the experiences of) a future colleague.

So far, your panel would consist of the direct manager and one peer of the candidate,

Who else? Well, if you're a large enough company and there is a H.R manager (or someone designated as such), then they would also likely attend.

So, who's missing? – at a stretch, maybe one of the manager's peers (another manager). Really? well, maybe, or maybe not. What would be the benefit of a second manager attending? - potentially another set of eyes and ears that can have a more relaxed approach (if they are not a direct stakeholder), and maybe provide some insights that you miss. Of course, for a larger company where your (management) candidate interacts with several existing managers, then at least one of those managers could join the panel.

But I'm now scraping around for more panel members, and this is our sign to stop. Refer back to the golden rule – if they have no direct purpose being there, then they shouldn't be on the panel.

So, this points to three and a maximum of four. Just make sure your candidate doesn't get this feeling:

Let's find you a friend!

One common issue with panels and especially when using a rectangular table for your interview (as this tongue-in-cheek picture shows), is that in a panel format, the panel members invariably all line up on one side. And that's an arrangement you should avoid.

If you only have a rectangular table available [30,] then someone needs to become the candidate's friend. It's a simple technique that goes a long way to making the candidate feel comfortable (and you know the rest – more relaxed = more to say and contribute).

The friend could logically be the direct manager (who we assume conducted – or was present, during the first interview).

The technique? – in a rectangular table layout, they sit on the same side as the candidate. The designated friend should also do the following:

- Introduce the other panel members, explaining their roles in the company.

---

30. *If you can locate a round table, use it for your panel interview. It imbues a sense of balance and equality which will help your candidate relax.*

- Effectively "chair" the panel interview by outlining the agenda/ purpose.
- Control the interview by keeping panel members on track with their questions.
- Ensure that all proposed questions by the panel members are relevant[31]

A better way

When it comes to panel interviews where two to four members will be on the panel, I have always recommended taking the interview out of the office. The reason is simple: It breaks the formality and lessens the likelihood of any intimidation. If your candidate isn't feeling intimidated, then I'll wager they at least feel a bit nervous or potentially not relaxed enough in their own minds to get all their points across (in an answer or a discussion). It's worth repeating ingredient number four: **Make your candidates feel comfortable**. In this way you get the most out of them.

An outside, neutral setting can really work to your advantage by keeping everyone relaxed. Remember a key point in the section on second interviews: You're always going to learn something new. Unless of course, the following happens:

---

31. *Unfortunately, some panel members ask particularly difficult (and sometimes largely irrelevant questions) to justify their position on the panel. The "friend" needs to be on the lookout for these.*

TALES FROM THE V🔑ULT

Just what did you hope to learn?

As if Seth didn't have a tough enough time in his interview with me, he bravely fronted up to his panel interview (his second with this employer) and well, where I went gently on the questions, one of the panel members delivered the most misguided question I had ever heard from an employer. I had convinced my client (let's call them ABC Bank) to conduct the interview off-site to de-formalize the event. A suitable coffee shop was located.

The three-person panel (excluding myself) comprised the senior manager, the middle-manager (whom Seth would report to if successful), and another employee who would be a colleague to Seth (peer). The interview began with several questions appropriate for an economist. Everything was going well, until the middle-manager unleashed the following question:

"If you suddenly found yourself with $20 million (courtesy of a lottery win), what would you then do with yourself?"

Seth responded that he had always dreamt of perfecting his recipe for steak, and would therefore open his own steak-based restaurant. He would of course, invest the remainder of the money in the type of shares ABC bank itself invests in.

The middle manager advised Seth that if **he won** $20 million, he would spend every waking hour trying to figure out how to turn the $20 million into $40 million.

Not only was Seth taken aback, but so was I and, crucially, so was the senior manager.

At first glance, you might think the issue at hand was how to explain to Seth that the question had no relevance, and how I would explain the same (diplomatically) to the middle-manager.

> But, of course, that wasn't the issue. The real issue was Seth's facial expression which said: "Would I really be working for this middle-manager, and what would that be like? Is it a wise career move to decline a job offer with a bank"?
>
> From my perspective, Seth's answer was exactly as it should have been. He gave an honest answer to a hypothetical question. I think we can all imagine resigning from our jobs if $20 million suddenly dropped into our bank account.
>
> Seth's answer also showed the entire panel (excluding the middle-manager) that Seth had a well-balanced outlook on life and work. A highly-strung economist working with hundreds of millions of dollars is not an ideal combination. Seth's answer got a tick from me, but the question got a big thumbs-down.

Seth's experience is a great example of why one panel member needs to establish the agenda, collate (and review) all the questions beforehand. It's also worth keeping in mind that a panel interview is still just an interview, and your candidate is evaluating you as their future employer, almost as much as you are evaluating them. You need to keep putting your best foot forward.

And the result? Seth's initial concerns were allayed, and he joined ABC bank, performed well, and enjoyed a solid and progressive career there.

The future of the middle-manager? He wasn't hired using the Secret Sauce method, and his unorthodox approach had already manifested itself in some strained internal relationships. He was an example of **Would do the job** but did not possess the right skills to **Do the job**. It was also clear as time marched on that he did not **Fit in**. ABC bank ultimately realized that.

Saying goodbye – rejecting candidates after an interview

When it comes time to reject an interviewed candidate – including those who have been reference checked, and/or undergone a psychometric assessment, then you're going to need an effective script to follow. Note that this subsection forms a pair with the section on rejecting after a psychometric assessment (Chapter 12).

Empathy is essential here. Consider that some candidates have been on an emotional journey through your hiring process. They may have believed they were just days away from landing their ideal job. Their sense of disappointment could be very real.

Against this backdrop, the most effective technique I have found is to talk in terms of the overall picture (of both the candidate, and your company).

The "overall picture" technique

In simple terms, this means not going down the path of discussing specific experiences, or individual skills. If you do, then you will be steering the discussion to where the candidate has the advantage (i.e.: their recall – and/or it becomes a subjective discussion), and away from where you want the discussion to go. The "what" of the discussion is about a non-alignment (with your company), that you know most about, and the candidate knows least about.

A little confused? I can't say I blame you. Here are the lines I have recanted hundreds of times before:

> *I/we (at the company) can certainly recognise your skills and experience (insert relevant example such as bookkeeping). Throughout this process, you have been one of two/three/four candidates who made it to interview/second interview/psychometric testing/reference checking.*
>
> *We've had some difficult decisions to make. In truth, there is not much separating any of you, and certainly, any of you could perform the role here.*
>
> *Ultimately, we've decided to move ahead with another candidate who we feel is a slightly better fit in relation to our company (its operating style).*

Now, providing you do have other candidates you are considering advancing (and you know where their specific skills/strengths are – versus those of this candidate), then a slight variation (or addition) on the script could be as follows:

> *We just felt the experience of one of the other candidates was better matched to our job vacancy. They had a little more of (insert specific skill-experience here), and this is what gave them the slight advantage.*

Stepping downwards

Up to now, we have assumed that the candidate you are about to reject is a high-quality candidate who did everything right, and very little wrong. If, however, the reality includes some of the issues raised in the Interview Masterclass series, then you could consider including those in your verbal rejection script – but perhaps tread gently here.

Further downwards still

While I wouldn't suggest using the following as your exclusive verbal script, you could consider adding it to the techniques (above).

I'm talking about verbally stated, or printed preferences, that are markedly different than your job role – e.g.: the candidate has listed a preference to work in a large company (100+ employees) where yours is much smaller - or perhaps a stated desire for a higher salary than you are offering, etc. I'm sure you get the picture. Know what their stated preferences are for certain areas, and know that they are clearly different to what either your job advert, or your job description outlines.

Summary

Performing some kind of sequel – some type of "encore" will deliver real benefits to your candidate evaluation, and it will most definitely help you stay connected to your preferred candidate, or your entire shortlist – and in some cases, just that alone can be enough. For each type of position (or job role) that you hire for, the exact make-up of your sequel may well be different, and that's fine.

Please consider.

Chapter 12

Now I see the real you
(Psychometric assessments)

It's not magic. It's science.

Chapter rating

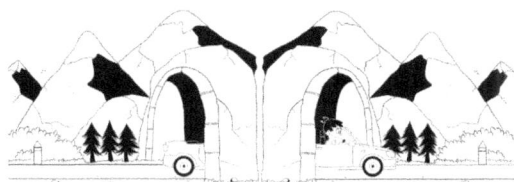

New discoveries await.

Let's begin this chapter with another **BIG** statement:

Psychometric assessments work – and they work so well, that if you don't use them, you're robbing yourself of some very powerful candidate insights[32].

I never proceed to the offer stage - for any candidate, without using one. Psychometrics is virtually a separate field in itself, so it can be easy to drift into excessive detail. We're going to avoid that by limiting our discussion to just the absolute need-to-know stuff. Here are the three main benefits to you as an employer:

1. Psychometric assessments can confirm your preferred candidate is the right person for you and your company - reinforcing the perceptions you've already gained through your interview(s). Another way of looking at this is to view psychometric assessments as powerful (and inexpensive) insurance.

2. They can prevent you from making a hiring mistake by uncovering undesirable personality traits which have been well-guarded up to this point.

3. You will almost always learn something new from your candidate's psychometric report. This can be a pleasing revelation of additional benefits the candidate can bring to your company. As an example, your candidate may have management potential, expanding the ways in which they can contribute to your organization long-term. You can then confirm these new findings via your reference checking (refer next chapter).

---

32. *This is providing you use a properly validated psychometric assessment. Refer to our website for access to internationally validated psychometric assessments.*

How do they work exactly?

Psychometric assessments are questionnaires framed around a wide variety of workplace scenarios. The questions are underpinned (in the case of hiring's secret sauce) by the many facets (traits) of the big five personality model discussed in Chapter 8.

In practice, a sponsoring employer[33] issues an email to their candidate(s) which includes a link. The candidate clicks on the link, answers the questionnaire, and a report is then automatically compiled and forwarded to the sponsoring employer. Quick, easy, and inexpensive. The entire process from start to finish can be less than one hour.

What's the value-add in using psychometric assessments?

Speed, accuracy, and depth, is the short answer here. More on this in a moment.

Recall in Chapter 8, we introduced the OCEAN model with its five principal domains to explain personality. These five principal domains are each comprised of three facets (giving organizational psychologists 15 facets in total to work with). Psychometric assessments use these facets to uncover how a specific candidate is likely to perform in the workplace.

Being able to assess candidates for their levels of productivity, teamwork, organizational skills, and initiative, are of considerable benefit in any job role, and for every employer.

For that reason, we've carefully selected a testing partner, and you can test your own candidates through our website.

Accuracy and depth were mentioned as to why psychometric assessments are so powerful.

Psychometric assessments are statistically validated for their accuracy, and they contain mechanisms inside their questioning, to remove bias in the way a given candidate might want to answer the questions (to appear more acceptable or capable). The depth aspect comes from the

33. *Employers can visit our website, download free sample reports, and then issue our big five psychometric assessment directly to their candidate(s).*

sheer number of personality facets that can be tested for, well inside one hour. It is certainly more than you could uncover and measure with just an interview alone.

Sceptical?

I've certainly encountered sceptical employers over the years. They generally fell into two groups. The first group weren't believers for whatever reason (and had not used psychometric assessments), and the second group had tried an assessment, but weren't convinced the results were accurate (up to that point).

What I can say, is that almost without fail, once the first group of employers begin to use psychometric assessments, they change their mind. In fact, many go on to become advocates for the science.

As for the second group, what was it that ultimately changed their thinking? Often, it was a time delay - the assessment report uncovered scores for certain traits which ran contra to the impressions the employer had gained at the interview. Perhaps an unstructured interview format had been used, or too much reliance on "gut instinct".

These employers questioned certain personality trait scores at the outset, but where they did proceed to hire, several months of employment subsequently verified those scores.

Were there good or bad "discoveries" made? I dare say they were turning a blind eye to some forewarnings in the assessment report. Being proven wrong is sometimes a bitter pill to swallow, and it took some time for those employers to adopt psychometric assessments into their hiring process – but most went on to do exactly that.

Do they have something to hide?

Just as there are believers and non-believers among employers, there are two types of candidates when it comes to psychometric assessments – the vast majority who are happy to participate, and the few who don't want to – but who ultimately participate after some coaxing. This second group represents 3% - 5% of candidates. You can probably guess why...

That's right – they're either unsure of themselves, or they're hiding something.

Luckily, with the percentage being so small, it's only rarely that you will encounter hesitation or pushback. What is essential to keep in mind is that just like all the other steps in the secret sauce, this is also a non-negotiable step.

But what happens when you encounter one of the "difficult" candidates?

Typically, after voicing their concerns or reason for hesitancy, they are very likely to undertake your assessment. Why is that? – It's because candidates are compliant and especially so, when nearing the final stages of a hiring exercise. They're mentally committed to your process, and generally don't want to risk missing a job offer.

However, the question remains: how will they approach their assessment?

Well, let's consider that psychometric assessments are based on multiple choice questions, or a choice between two statements.

A typical example is as follows:

Question 1: It can be necessary to sacrifice perfection for efficiency (choose one)
Strongly disagree ☐ Disagree ☐ Slightly disagree ☐ Slightly agree ☐ Agree ☐ Strongly agree ☐
Question 2: (Select either statement)
Honesty is always the best policy ☐ Sometimes telling a white lie is necessary to achieve a result ☐

There are typically 150 or more questions like this, taking around 20 – 40 minutes to answer.

The vast majority of candidates are happy to participate and will answer the questions honestly. You (the employer) then receive an accurate candidate report.

Too smart by half?

Among the difficult group, there are some who (unfortunately) attempt to read into the intent of the questions – to discern their purpose or "aim" if you will.

These individuals misunderstand the intention of these questions, and the resulting report may be inaccurate in one or more areas. Our recommended psychometric assessment advises you if a candidate has answered dishonestly, but it's not what you want to see happen.

Consider this following candidate (Adrian) from an earlier hiring exercise:

TALES FROM THE VULT

How to shoot yourself in the foot.

I was closing out a hiring exercise for a client (ABC Automation). The preferred candidate (Adrian) had just completed his psychometric assessment. The problem was that Adrian's scores for certain personality traits were noticeably different from what we had come to understand through our two interviews. The assessment report had also flagged that Adrian had answered some questions dishonestly, and recommended reviewing the results carefully.

As I sat down with Adrian to ask what happened, the discussion inevitably arrived at the point where he admitted answering certain questions dishonestly, in the hope of appearing more impressive than he actually was.

I explained the position he had just placed us all in.

In short, we now had three options. The first option was to suggest that he had made some innocent mistakes when answering the questionnaire. This would involve me lying to ABC Automation. That wasn't going to happen.

The second option was admitting that Adrian deliberately answered some questions dishonestly, in a misguided attempt to improve his scores in the report. Under this scenario, ABC Automation would be asked to employ an admitted liar.

That wasn't going to happen either.

The third option was that ABC Automation could ask Adrian to do the assessment again, but the question over why he lied the first time around, would always be present.

The outcome? Adrian was disqualified from the hiring exercise. An almost certain job offer with a great employer had slipped through his fingers.

Dishonesty in a hiring exercise is always a bad outcome and if ever you encounter it, well, it can't be overlooked. If this happens to you, just re-engage with the other candidates on your shortlist (your top 2-4 candidates) or go back and advertise again.

So right here is another important tip - candidate management. Back in Chapter 5 we spoke about sensitively rejecting unsuccessful candidates, and here we're outlining the importance of regular contact with your shortlisted candidates, until your employment contract has been signed. Up until that point, you may need to come back to your shortlist. Adrian's case shows that.

Psychometric assessments improve your reference checking

Your candidate report will often deliver additional insights which may be unexpected (hopefully in a good way). Some of these new insights may simply be a higher or lower score for a particular trait (let's assume for teamwork).

In the secret sauce reference check, there is an area for custom questions. Be sure to add those new surprise areas in the form of specific questions for your referees. Let's assume your candidate (let's call him Michael) scored on the low side for teamwork, but there was nothing detected during your interview.

A custom question would be as follows:

"We have a specific question over Michael's teamwork orientation. We're not sure that teamwork is a particular strength for Michael. What has been your experience and importantly, what have you witnessed in this regard?"

Do you share the assessment results?

Once the assessment has been completed, you're going to find yourself in possession of a very powerful document. One that likely provides additional insights to your candidate. The practical outcome of this is that *you* are empowered, but your candidate is *not*.

Your candidate is (understandably) going to be just as interested as you are in learning what's inside the report.

My advice is *not to share a copy* of the assessment report with the candidate, but rather talk to them in an overall sense about the report's findings. As an example, you might say that *the report supports the views and opinions already formed about you - from our interview and other interactions.* Alternatively, you might make a general statement that you're happy with the report's findings however, the company owns the report, and it is company policy not to provide copies to candidates.

I do however recommend that if the candidate is hired, that you share the findings (but not provide them with a copy), after successful completion of their probationary period (typically 3 - 6 months). This timeline says to the candidate (employee) that you are happy with their performance regardless of whether there were any causes for concern flagged in their report.

It's also worth remembering that until your reference checking has been completed (which will help support or question the assessment findings), you are unlikely to have a fully formed opinion of your candidate. Information sharing at this stage isn't warranted.

What about the other possibility? Rejecting after an assessment

This certainly requires some finesse...

To reject a preferred candidate after their assessment means that the report uncovered some personality (trait) scores that were unacceptable to you. That might be for something you rate as being important in your company e.g.: planning and organizing. And of course, it's possible the report uncovered some completely new information for you – perhaps that your candidate scored far too low for teamwork, or maybe that they scored below your expectations in several other key personality traits.

If you haven't read the sample script for rejecting candidates following interviews, then you should start there (Chapter 11).

Past this, you have two possible scenarios.

The first is that you only tested one candidate (let's call them the preferred candidate) and the second is that you tested your entire shortlist (i.e.: your top 2 - 4 candidates who were all interviewed).

If it's the latter we're dealing with, then you can rest more on the interview rejection script found in Chapter 11 — i.e.: we simply had a preference for one of the other shortlisted candidates.

If it was a single tested candidate then realistically, any rejection that occurs soon after completing their assessment, is going to be obvious to them.

Firstly, pre-prepare your job - candidate specific talking points, then talk to your candidate in terms of their overall *(evaluation)* picture. In other words, you have to necessarily take the focus off their psychometric assessment results, and discuss the overall picture that you have formed of them. In practice, it might sound like this:

"We have waited until you completed the psychometric assessment, so that we could compare it to the impressions we gained of you at interview — and all the way back to our initial telephone/videoconferencing screening. We're happy that everything lines up quite well. We've held some internal discussions to see how well you compare to our job vacancy and also, our company's operating style, (omit if not relevant), and how well we think the job matches your specific skills and preferences.

Overall, we're not certain that both sides are an ideal fit for each other. While it's possible we may think differently about this later on, for the moment, we think it's best for both sides to disengage.

We understand that this is probably not the answer you want, however we've put a lot of thought into our decision, and hope you can understand our viewpoint".

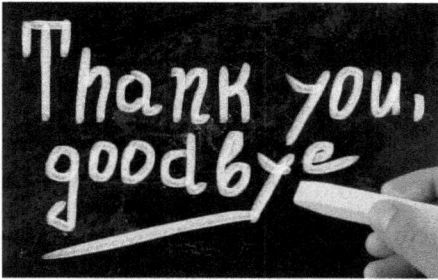

Delivering a verbal rejection is never easy, and your candidate may want to probe further but essentially, you've got to back yourself on this. Basically, no means no.

Summary

Psychometric assessments are an invaluable and easy-to-add tool[34] to your hiring process. This makes them an absolutely essential part of hiring's secret sauce. Apply it just for your preferred candidate to confirm your impressions, or your shortlist (top 2 - 4 candidates), to help separate them. But just do it. You'll be so glad you did.

Pre-employment medical checks (somebody call a doctor!)

This isn't so much a Hiring Secret Sauce step or even an ingredient, but it is a strong recommendation. In fact, it's almost a given now for every hiring exercise I'm involved in. First, a little bit of background...

Pre-employment medical checks are something I initially used for trade and operational roles, where the new employee would be working in a factory, or out on a project site. They proved their value to me when they were applied to a role for an earthmoving machinery driver (picture one of those vehicles where the tires are taller than you are). This was for the construction of a new highway. We were about to hire a particular candidate (driver) until he subsequently failed his pre-employment medical. He failed because the medical check included a

---

34. *Refer to our website to access our assessment partner and their fully validated, easy-to-use assessment.*

urine test, and the results showed traces of methamphetamine. Still other candidates (drivers) tested positive for alcohol abuse.

As time went on, I began adopting these medical checks for white-collar, professional roles. Just one of the reasons for that, is the increasing number of people who are abusing alcohol and other drugs. Alcohol dependent individuals can cause problems in managerial roles as easily as they can in trade level roles. And if we consider just the physical side, then new employees with unannounced back problems can suddenly require significant unplanned time away from their jobs.

Now, wherever your company is based, there may be laws dictating what can be tested for, so this advice is generic. You should check on the availability (and legality) of these pre-employment medical tests for your particular location.

A typical pre-employment medical test is divided into two sections. The first is a self-declaration (checklist) which the candidate completes before the medical assessment.

The checklist covers all pre-existing conditions ranging from the need for cardiac medications, through to injuries (which may, or may not, limit their ability to perform your particular job role). A benefit here is that falsifying their medical history and conditions may provide you with coverage if they subsequently cause performance issues.

When to apply

Pre-employment medical assessments are best applied here – immediately after a psychometric assessment, and before reference checking. There are a couple of good reasons for this.

The first reason is that similar to psychometric assessments, the subsequent report may contain delicate information (in some cases, much more sensitive than the report from a psychometric assessment). At the very least, it contains information of a confidential nature.

Secondly, pre-employment medicals will cost more than a psychometric assessment, and they will use up a reasonable amount of the candidate's time (certainly more than a psychometric assessment). So, on a cost basis alone, you probably want to limit these pre-employment medicals to just the candidate you intend to offer the job to.

On that basis though, why wouldn't you leave the medical until after the reference checking? The reason is simple: if it uncovers information which means you do not want to employ this particular candidate, then you shouldn't make the pre-employment medical the last step in your recruitment process – i.e.: a rejection at that point is too obvious.

Once you've undertaken this recommended (and beneficial) step, you have everything you need to move onto the final, key stage, of the hiring process.

Chapter 13

We know who your friends are

(The not-so-subtle art of reference checking)

Friends can't help your candidate here. Only those that actually worked with them will matter.

Chapter rating

A wild, fun ride – but hold onto your hat!

At the very beginning I said that Chapter 1 was critical (setting up your Job Description). It's also hard to go past Chapter 9 (Interviewing) – getting a good look inside your candidate for the first time.

But if there's another chapter that's just as important as those two, then it would have to be this one. It's that independent (third-party) verification that your candidate can, (and will), do what you need them to do.

These third parties can also confirm claimed achievements and provide critical insight as to whether your job opportunity is the right fit for your preferred candidate. In truth, reference checking is mostly about ingredient number nine – **Past performance is the best indicator of future performance**. It's one of the best tools we have for this, but it does a few other things for us as well...

You don't want to encounter this. All the referees must be in agreement about your candidate.

In Chapter 5, we looked at how to scrutinize claimed achievements during phone screening – by covering off the typical lies and exaggerations heard from candidates. And in Chapter 7, we looked at how these lies and embellishments are increasingly found in candidate resumés and online bio's.

Reference checking can see aspects of both those chapters come together – but applied to these third-party individuals (referees) that you've never met - and likely never will. And herein lies a clue as to where we will be going in this chapter but for now, let's get with the reference check process – what it is, and how to do it. Of course, you're going to need a reference check proforma[35]. It's half of the reference check procedure. The other half is the method outlined in this chapter.

"*We know who your friends are*" was chosen as this Chapter title because it addresses one of the common concerns about reference checking. The more skeptical employers out there will often say to me "aren't the referees all just friends of the candidate"?

Friends or impartial referees? You'll find out either way, and it won't matter.

While personal friends are never acceptable as work referees, we could perhaps refer to many referees as friendly colleagues and ex-colleagues. Now this in itself isn't necessarily a problem, because as you'll see, it's really about the second part of the chapter title – i.e., the not-so-subtle art of...

Let's begin by considering who the referees should be.

---

35. *The Secret Sauce Reference Check Proforma can be found on our website www.hiringsecretsauce.com*

Who's calling the shots here?

The first point to make is this: Your candidate won't be choosing who their referees are – *you* will. This means it won't matter what their personal relationship is, or isn't, with your candidate. It's whether they had the *right* working relationship with your candidate - and it's only if they did, that they will be able to answer the questions in the Reference Check Proforma. Because this document forms part of a three-way system with the Interview and Initial Screening Proformas, any inconsistencies will spell problems for your candidate – and that's the way it *has* to be. An example follows shortly.

So, the first component of the Secret Sauce method is you (The Employer) deciding the list of referees, and the second part is using the proforma. The proforma will ensure you apply some of the existing ingredients - specifically, ingredient number ten – **Deconstruct. Dig deeper. Demand details** along with ingredient number seven - **Can they do the job, will they do the job** *and***, will they fit in?**

Let's hope they get their story straight...

From the moment your candidate submitted their resumé to you, they made claims about their previous job roles – specifically, their job title(s), what they did, how long they did it for, and who they worked with - and for.

While I promised no stats, graphs, or big data, we can certainly look at a typical organizational chart. You'll need to draw one or more of these during your interview with the candidate[36] – following their advice on who they reported to, - and if your candidate was at supervisory level or above, who in turn, reported to them. This is a "*must do*" as it underpins a good part of the reference check.

---

36. *You will find ready-to-complete organizational charts in both our interview and reference check proformas.*

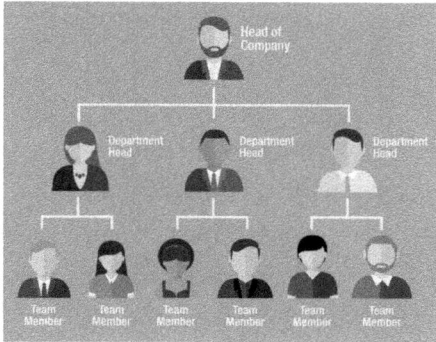

Draw a simple organizational chart showing where your candidate is placed, along with their job title and their immediate relationships (by using lines to join the different employees and their job functions together)

As we know from Chapters 5 and 9, your phone screening and interview uses their previous employment – their skills, achievements, duties, and responsibilities, as the basis for your evaluation (how well they compare to your job description). And logically enough, this extends to their referees corroborating those claims.

But I'm getting ahead of myself. This first part is about referee selection – just who exactly needs to be a referee and why.

Who makes the referee list?

The referee list is fundamentally shaped by the organizational chart(s) as advised by your candidate – during the interview[37]. Go back to your completed interview proforma and review their job roles and relationships within that company. Starting with their most recent employment, and by drawing their name and job title in a box, you would have asked them who they reported to, and who was on a similar level to them in that company (i.e.: the other employees on that same level who might be performing similar or even different jobs, but who would likely know your candidate). In addition, if your candidate has any direct reports of their own, these employees should also have been drawn in. If organizational charts weren't drawn up at the time of their interview, then talk to your candidate and do it now.

---

37. *Keep in mind the Dirty Dozen lies sometimes found in resumé's. Look to all your referee types to help verify the actual role and position your candidate held in the company. If your candidate claims they reported directly to the C.E.O well, is that true? or were they a bit lower down on the company organizational chart?*

Generally speaking, referees (three minimum) are drawn from the following:

1. A manager that the candidate reported directly to. If, for example, the candidate has reported to four different managers in four separate jobs, then the most recent manager is your preferred choice. The exception to this rule is when their most recent reporting relationship was, or is, short (let's say one year), but they reported to their second most recent manager for several years. This is an overarching rule with referee selection – that the most recent relationships are the most relevant. Imagine talking to the very first manager your candidate reported to when they were just beginning their working life, and they only stayed in that job for one year. Now imagine that same candidate has ten years total experience. They logically developed their skills over that timeframe. Recent experience is therefore better/best.

   The caveat here is that if your candidate is presently employed and working under their current manager, then it is unlikely that manager can be used as a referee. In these cases, the second most recent manager is your choice.

2. Next is a peer, a colleague, or an internal customer of the candidate. Talking to a peer or a colleague provides a different perspective on your candidate. You're looking for that peer or colleague to confirm your candidate's responsibilities, who they reported to, and what their widely acknowledged achievements and skills are. You will also learn how well they interact with other employees at their same level. Another great option to consider is an internal customer.

   This doesn't mean your candidate is working in sales. Almost every employee performs work which impacts on another employee (or several). Imagine an employee who writes software for a company, and then sends that software to the manufacturing department.

This makes the person in the manufacturing department an internal customer. How reliable is your candidate in meeting their deliverables? Are they easy to communicate with, etc.?

3. And, for those candidates who have one or more direct reports, at least one of the referees needs to be a direct report. How were they as a manager? Were they inclusive, or directive in their management style? Were they a good leader and communicator?

4. The fourth and final choice is an external contact such as a supplier (or for sales roles), an external customer. How well did your candidate perform their role in the eyes of an external contact? Did they represent their employer well? Were they fair and honest in all their dealings?

Can't come up with the referees?

We now know who the referees should be, but what if your candidate can't produce those referees? Let's assume they cannot produce referee type number 1 (manager) – or at least the specific manager you would like to talk to.

Where this occurs, you will need to move backwards through their work history, until you find another relevant Type 1 referee.

To keep things complicated for a moment, let's assume this is their second job and they're still employed there (meaning they can't ask their current manager to be a referee). And what if their previous (first) manager is either unavailable or unwilling to act as a referee? What then? Well, you could have an issue on your hands. Managers are the number one referee choice because logically enough, they are the ones best placed to confirm or contradict all the items you need to check.

Let's continue down the problem path. What if they can't produce a type 1 referee (manager) at all? Or they can't produce quality referees across types 1 to 4. What do you do now? What are your options moving ahead?

From experience, it's a rare occurrence when you're dealing with a quality candidate. By *quality*, I mean one who presented a solid work history (in their resumé), performed well during phone screening and interview (and would have also produced a solid result on their psychometric assessment).

The bottom line is that while rare for a quality candidate, if you are placed in a position where the candidate cannot field the right type and number of referees, then you should disengage from that candidate. That's right, you should let them go.

Sounds like a big call to make, but where reference checks have been compromised in this way, a poor hire often occurs. It must be said that it is normally found alongside a hiring process with a less-than-robust interview, and quite likely, no psychometric assessment.

Think about it this way. Some and perhaps many of their claimed achievements, along with their past job tenure (who they worked for, the duration, the role they had, etc.), can't be independently verified. Or at least, significant parts of their work history can't be verified. That's a risk you probably don't want to take.

What do you actually want?

Simple. You want the candidate to forward the right referees (the most suitable mix of type 1 to 4 referees), and you want those referees to be able to answer all the questions in your reference check proforma. It's not too much to ask, is it? – just have the referees prove the candidate worked the jobs they claimed to have worked, for the nominated employer, during the times specified, etc.

This should (and will) be your experience 50% - 70% of the time.

What? I hear you ask. Why isn't that number higher? Why wouldn't it be 90% plus?

Asking the questions in our reference check proforma is straight-forward enough. Getting the expected answers? – unfortunately less so. Let's draw on some real-life examples...

TALES FROM THE VAULT

Not really who you said you were?

I thought the question was straightforward enough, but sure, I'll repeat it:

"What would you regard as the best project that Ryan delivered while he was a Project Manager at ABC Electricity Company?

Well, it's kind of hard to say, came the reply.

As per usual, I remain completely silent on the other end of the phone. I give no clues - no easy "out" to the referee.

I'm talking to Jeremy (Ryan's referee) who finally says – "do you have a project of Ryan's that you would like me to comment on"?

I reply that no, I don't (I do actually but I'm not saying). "I just wanted your recollection of a standout project of Ryan's.

This isn't going well with Jeremy, which means it's about to go badly for Ryan. You see, I'm scoring Jeremy's answers on my reference check proforma, and comparing them with the answers and scores from Ryan's interview – and they're just not lining up.

I'm about to tell Ryan that Jeremy could not corroborate his claimed work achievements. So, who's lying here? – because someone almost certainly is about something. At its completion, I advise Ryan that the reference check with Jeremy was unsatisfactory. It transpired that Ryan was operating at a slightly lower level than he claimed, and Jeremy didn't have the oversight of Ryan's work as he claimed. Ryan was subsequently overlooked for one of the other candidates on the shortlist.

While we're on a roll, let's take a look at another unusual reference check…

TALES FROM THE V🔑ULT

They just didn't like each other.

I've got what I suspect is a "dud" list of referees. The first referee couldn't give me the fine details I wanted, but it's this second referee that is turning this exercise on its head.

Suffice to say that referee number two has been giving subtle clues that he doesn't care much for the candidate. This is unusual, but not unheard of.

It really starts to go downhill when the referee suggests that considering this candidate for our job vacancy would result in the candidate "not being happy in such a job" and very likely to leave in a short period of time.

Referee number two goes on to play down the claimed achievements of the candidate, explaining that others contributed to the results without providing any real proof to support that statement.

Following this reference check, I decide to go back to referee number one who also works in the same company as referee number two.

Referee one advises me that the candidate and referee number two were both in line for the same promotion two years earlier. The candidate got the promotion and referee number two has clearly despised him ever since.

Why would the candidate offer number two as a referee, and why did number two agree to be a referee? It's simple really. It turns out that the candidate never really gave any thought to referee two's feelings after the promotion issue, and referee two clearly kept his feelings to himself – until now. It's also due to my requesting this exact person through my interview and reference check proformas (based on their organizational chart). Sometimes, candidates just don't do their own homework when it comes to referee selection. It happens.

Coaching, cheating or both?

Ryan and Jeremy are a good example of when people (both candidates and referees) are perhaps not who, or what, they claim to be. Was it deliberate? Well, that would mean…

Coaching of the referees…

This is perhaps one issue that won't come as a surprise to most employers – the concept that your candidate might attempt to coach the referees (to give the desired answers).

Let's preface this by saying that your candidate does need to contact the selected referees to confirm their availability to take your call. While they're at it, you should encourage your candidate to provide the referee with some background as to the job role they are pursuing with your company. That's because at a certain point, you're going to explain to the referee what your job vacancy is all about – and you're going to discuss with the referee if (and why) your job role would be a good fit for the candidate.

I don't want to make too much of this last point because what happens in practice is the Secret Sauce proforma will build a picture for you based on all the referees' answers. In other words, this important question will answer itself across the reference check.

Now, back to the coaching part…

As we saw with the Ryan and Jeremy example, it is easy to unmask a referee or candidate that is clearly not on the same page as you, but from experience, any fakery (coaching) is usually more subtle. Generally, it's around tenure, actual job titles and responsibilities, or one's true position on the organizational chart (candidate or referee). Once more, we're back to where you built up the organizational chart. We just need to take one more step.

It's a step that helps us cut through any referee coaching (or faking) and it's the **thirteenth ingredient in the Secret Sauce:**

HIRING'S SECRET SAUCE   **RRR – Remember to Reference check the Referees.**

You might be inclined to accept (on face value) that the referee is who they claim to be. But would it shock you to learn that some referees aren't exactly who they claim to be?

And of course, if your candidate says that Mr John Smith was their previous manager (whom they reported to between May 2020 and March 2024), then you'd be inclined to believe them. But should you believe them, is the real question here.

Up to this point, Hiring's Secret Sauce has likely imbued in you a healthy skepticism when it comes to dealing with candidates.

It's a mindset really. A mindset that requires solid proof to be shown to you. That mindset must now extend to referees. Without continuing this same mindset for referees, there's a risk this all-important reference check step can be compromised. I'm going to step way-over the average challenge when it comes to this **RRR** concept by introducing you to the extreme end of **RRR**.

This final surprise is potentially waiting for you out there. It exists. It's wrong on several levels, and I remain convinced it's against the law. It's all in the title.

Liars for hire

How to break this to you? I don't think there's an easy way, so let's just jump straight in.

The concept of referees being coached by the candidate is nothing new. However, a more recent development has been the emergence of companies that can be hired to act as completely false referees – right down to fabricating an alternative work history for you.

It's unlikely your candidate would engage such a service, but they might emulate parts of it.

These companies will create an alternative resumé for you, and they have actors that will play the role of your particular referee. It's a world of deception and misinformation – for a price. Some go as far as creating telephone numbers with the same area code for the region that the fake referee (supposedly) lives or works in.

The last thing I'm going to do is to give any of them a free plug by mentioning them by name but trust me, they do exist and worse still, some candidates claim to have landed well-paid jobs using these services. If that's true, then I doubt they went through a robust hiring process.

Fortunately, you can cut through their lies by using the Secret Sauce Reference Check and Interview proformas. You need to use these two processes together because it's the continuity and depth of detail, that the *liars for hire* will struggle with.

Let's also keep in mind that any candidate who would use such a service or even coach a referee to falsify information, deserves to be found out and disqualified[38].

One of your main strategies to overcome these *liars for hire* (and it really is a non-negotiable) is that you request the landline phone numbers of the referees, along with the street address of the business they claim to work at (either at the same company as the candidate, or if

---

38. *This last point is important and its why you will find advice on how to protect your company in Chapter 14 "Landing your fish".*

they're now working elsewhere – then at their new company/location). This is the first part of **RRR**.

On your computer, use Google to confirm the street address, and then dial the **main switchboard number** shown under the Google company entry. Take this one step further by using Google maps to positively identify the company's physical location. Then phone and ask for the referee by name. Confirm that they still work there – or did work there and confirm their job title. This holds up for any referee claiming to still be employed by that company – and possibly even for a referee that departed that company not so long ago.

Some of these *liar for hire* groups claim to offer 200 or more fictional companies from which to create their fake work histories. This is why the Google maps approach works – fictional companies don't occupy real buildings visible using the street view in Google. Nor do they have tangible products or services that you can identify.

If you're attempting to talk to a referee from some years back in the candidate's work history, then there's a chance they're no longer employed there. This is where the second part of RRR comes into play:

Supporting documentation (on the referee)

Any type 1 referee (Manager) should be able to provide you with some form of identification. This doesn't mean their driver's license rather, it means a business card, company letter, or an email address. In other words, something that proves they are (or were) a manager in that particular company. In fact, ask for two items of identification.

As a prompt, you can explain that your company has upgraded its reference check procedure – nothing personal, but referees are now required to provide proof of claimed tenure, and proof of the claimed relationship to the candidate. A genuine referee should be happy to comply.

Any risk here is on you, and your hiring process. If you want to forego this identification process, then you have to accept some risk.

For certain referee types, it may be a little difficult to obtain this professional identification, but you should still try. It's well worth the effort.

A written statement can act as a real disincentive for that referee to lie.

Once you've verified the referee's (employment) identity, it's then on to conducting the reference check by using the proforma.

Some recommended techniques (referee authentication).

There are four techniques I recommend you use with referees.

The first is to ask the referee to describe the organizational chart to you – the same one you drew during your interview (including the names of the surrounding employees). Can they do it? If not, why not? Surely a type 1 referee could populate that organizational chart as accurately as your candidate.

Second, ask the referee to describe the candidate – both in terms of their physical appearance, and their personality (How would they describe the candidate to others – their attributes and personality traits?). Does it match with the person you interviewed?

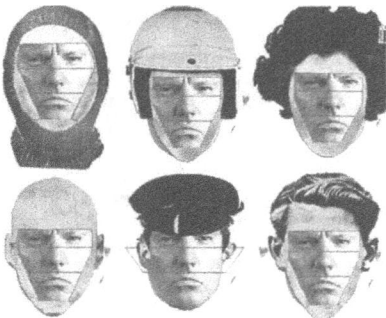

Third. When discussing the achievements of the candidate, ask the referee to expand by identifying (name and job titles) of other colleagues who were involved – or benefitted from, the achievement.

Fourth. Discuss some of the products or services the candidate worked with (or simply those of the company), during that specific work tenure. You can obtain this background from the candidate and confirm it via a small amount of Internet research yourself. Could you find the company (and perhaps their website), and do those products/services exist? A referee should be on the same page when it comes to these products or services. Ask the referee to talk about products A & B (etc.).

Job done?

Your endgame here are referees that can answer the questions on your reference check proforma. They should be able to corroborate all the claimed work history – i.e.: achievements, tenures (start and finish dates), job title and organizational chart details (where all those small lines connect to and from).

A pass means almost perfect alignment between resumé content, phone screening, interview notes, psychometric test results and the reference check.

In truth, working with quality candidates should mean that your reference check process is near seamless. No surprises there.

And assuming you achieve this, then it is job done and you're on your way to the final stage – The Offer Stage.

Chapter 14
Landing your fish
(The offer stage)

Chapter rating

At journey's end – almost!

Back in Chapter 2 we used the analogy of attracting candidates in the same way you would attract fish. This chapter is all about landing your fish – because well, you haven't landed them yet – it's not a "done deal". We're going to delve into the mindset of candidates as they receive an offer of employment, and provide you with several effective techniques for extending your offer successfully, and landing your fish. And of course, there's always that other possibility – that during the offer stage, you realise you've hooked an undesirable fish, and you need to let them go. It's rare, but it does happen.

What could possibly go wrong?

Keep this.

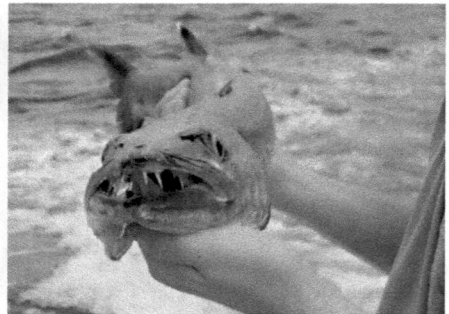

Let this one go.

No surprises please

The big takeaway here is that 90% of the failures to secure your new employee, come back to the Job Description in Chapter 1. During my first year in recruitment, I failed several times to secure the new employee. I finally realized it was because I pushed forward with the hiring exercise, without addressing up-front, where the candidate stood in relation to the key responsibilities of the job role, their qualifications (and desire) to perform that role, plus several smaller issues (which included the wage/salary on offer). Once I learnt to address those issues up-front (during phone screening and interview), what remained was only a 10% chance that I would fail to secure that new employee (more on that later).

In simple terms, it's surprises on either side (the candidate or employer) that cause the offer stage to slide off the rails.

In Chapter 1, I also mentioned that the J.D should form the central part of your employment contract – given that your candidate was phone screened, interviewed and reference checked against your J.D. During the interview, you would have shown the candidate your completed J.D and talked them through the main responsibilities of the job.

Your candidate now (rightfully) expects the employment contract to be all about delivering on the responsibilities and duties listed in your J.D. And providing it does, you can be reasonably comfortable about things.

And If for any reason there's been a change in that document (in other words, exactly what the job role is going to be about) then you need to address it now.

The Secret Sauce J.D template includes the salary on offer – it's a key point. Your salary offer (and the expectations of the candidate) needed to be covered during your interview.

"No surprises" must be the mantra from your side and, it needs to be from the candidate side as well – because this is where most of the 10% outside of your control comes from.

Let's look at the four main issues that contribute to the 10% of failures. The last two issues are interrelated:

1. You lost out to a better opportunity

A different offer which they preferred more. It's not about being quicker.

In truth there is not much you can do about this one – nor should you.

You might find that a strange statement to make, but just consider the following:

If you've adhered to the Secret Sauce method, then you were thorough and put your best foot forward. There can be a number of reasons why your candidate prefers an alternative job to yours, but it's unlikely to be because they didn't understand what your job entailed. You can (and likely will), sit down with them one more time to cover off your J.D and the benefits of joining your company. But the chances are, it won't change things.

During your interview, you would have enquired about any other jobs they were pursuing. We know from Chapter 4 that great talent doesn't wait around, so it's not surprising that they may be at the offer stage elsewhere, and they're weighing up which one is best for them. If your salary offer is competitive, it's likely to come down to preferences that are very hard (maybe even impossible) for you to compete with. Think: slightly different (more preferred) duties and responsibilities, different products and/or services, shorter commute times etc. In other words, the two jobs are different and that's out of your control.

2. Show me your papers.

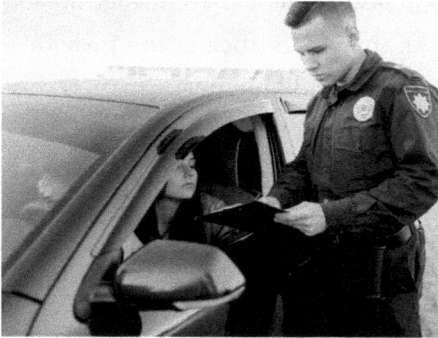

As drivers, we must prove we have a license before we are allowed on the road.

Obtaining confirmation of a candidate's claimed academic qualifications and relevant licenses (such as a driver's license or a forklift license) or any other qualification required to perform the job on offer, is something you absolutely need to do.

In Chapter 7 we read about the case of an employee with his partially faked qualifications, and we listed the "Dirty Dozen" – the most common lies encountered with candidates and their resumé content.

Although it's unusual to be lied to at this late stage of proceedings, it does occasionally happen. The percentage? – around 5% to 10% across all job types[39].

Personally, I sight the qualifications and licenses of candidates at, or following, their interview, but for most of you, it's going to feel a lot more natural to leave it to this point in proceedings.

As the Secret Sauce method was designed primarily for white collar employees, let's look at the most common issues I encounter with that group:

1. The candidate studied marketing at University X, but didn't see it through to the end, and graduate. They may have completed 80% of the coursework but for obvious reasons, they can't produce their degree (where university degrees or diplomas are involved, you need to sight those qualifications).

---

39. *Based on my agency experience over the last 20 years.*

For those who did graduate and can produce a copy of their degree, I strongly recommend you also request their academic transcript. These are harder to fake than a certificate, and provide important insights as to whether their academic performance was excellent, average, or below average.

2. *"I certainly graduated, but having moved house several times, I can no longer locate said degree/diploma etc."*. This is the adult version of "the dog ate my homework" and usually just as credible. It's a simple matter of asking them to contact the institution involved and request a certified copy (a common request in academia).

3. The age of the candidate is not as they have suggested during the hiring exercise (this may or may not be an issue for you). Request a copy of their driver's license.

4. Claim to hold a university degree, when in fact it is a diploma (this is a generic example of over-claiming).

5. For candidates born outside your country and claiming (for example) qualifications in engineering, those qualifications need to be assessed by your country's relevant industry or governing body. Insist on sighting these local assessments. In any professional field, this can be a restriction on working, or potentially, working illegally.

6. For candidates born overseas, relevant residency VISA status/ citizenship etc.

7. Other reasons for not being permitted to work in your industry. This seems like a broad statement to make but just as an example, most finance industry jobs require proof that the candidate has never been bankrupt, and has no criminal record.

So, an inability to produce (or falsified) qualifications, licenses, approvals, VISA status etc., are a contributing factor in the 5% to 10% of failures.

3. Cold feet

It's a bit late to be getting cold feet, but it does happen.

Alternatively known as a change of heart, getting cold feet can often be overcome by you (the employer). This is especially true where the cold-feet sensation has been generated by the candidate themselves, rather than say, their current employer (that's the next point).

It may be surprising that cold feet would come up at this very late stage, but on occasion that's exactly what happens. Even though your candidate may currently be employed, the majority (of these cold-feet candidates) will not announce to their current employer, that they are thinking of leaving or indeed, have received an offer of employment elsewhere.

In other words, things are just between you and them at this stage (thankfully). When I encounter cold feet, it's usually because the candidate has worked at their existing place of employment for quite some time. They like their colleagues and well, they're very comfortable in what they do there. They may also have good reason to believe that their current employment is very secure, and security of tenure is a major hold for many employees.

Let's now look at the related issue 4, before we consider what you can do about cold feet.

4. Receiving a counteroffer from their existing employer

So, now you want me to stay?

The percentages here differ greatly but from my experience, around 40% of candidates receive some form of counteroffer from their current employer (when they advise they are leaving for another opportunity).

Of the 40%, around three-quarters of those candidates quickly pour cold water on the idea. You've done your work well in adhering to all the Secret Sauce steps. There are no surprises coming your way. The candidate is switched on to your opportunity. They can't wait to join and come on board!

For that remaining percentage though, either a sense of loyalty, strong friendships or perhaps an offer of increased salary (maybe even a promotion), will get them thinking about staying.

There are some definite (and effective) techniques you can use when dealing with a candidate who has been counter-offered.

To explain what they are, we first need to deviate just for a moment, to look at how you extend your job offer, because it's central to your prospects of success.

Forget email and the postal service

If you post or email your contract of employment to your preferred candidate, then you're going to miss out on the single most important piece of feedback you can obtain – the look on their face as they read through the contract's main points (duties, responsibilities, salary etc.).

You're hoping for this reaction.

You really need to see this in person as you step through the main points of your employment contract. Along with a smile, they should be nodding their head in agreement as you step through the responsibilities list (which they would recall from their interview). If you're getting this reaction, then its job done!

And don't forget to review their salary / wage, working hours, holiday entitlements and any other perks of joining your company.

Now, just imagine instead that you emailed or posted out your employment contract. Somewhere – perhaps when they've opened the email, or walked back inside from their letterbox, they've run through the employment contract and hopefully, they still have the reaction shown above.

But let's imagine for a moment that they reacted like this:

It's usually minor, but it could be major. Never do it by remote.

Whatever it is (and possibly it's just a minor point), you really need to be in the room at this time. If you emailed it, there's a reasonable chance that the first person they talked to about their concerns wasn't you.

You've given up the ability to find out what it is that concerns them. Perhaps 90% of the offer is fine, but there are one or two points they are no longer sure about.

That's why you need to be in the room whichever way their initial reaction goes.

It's OK. We're friends now...

Once again, in person[40], is the only way you should be dealing with cold feet or a counteroffered candidate. That's because you're going to need to use empathy and influence (in that order), to handle the discussions.

It's worth repeating that if the candidate is fully switched on to your opportunity, then it's unlikely they will be swayed to remain with their current employer.

Let's start with Issue 3 (cold feet).

For the most part, these candidates are happy with their current job, and quite likely, with both their employer and existing work colleagues. In other words, there's a comfort level that you need to overcome.

---

40.   *If for any reason you can't do this in person, then try connecting via an Internet video call.*

The best approach is to revisit their reasons for applying to your job vacancy (which you would have captured on your interview proforma). In essence, it was likely to be one or more of the following:

- Their current job no longer represents a challenge (and your vacancy does).
- They see no obvious career path with their current employer.
- Their current employer is not experiencing growth (or may even be in decline).
- The products - services of their current employer are no longer appealing.
- Their salary – wage may be below what your vacancy is offering.

While there can be more reasons than these, remember that this is still about cold feet – there's something about their current situation, and it could well be about relationships or a comfort level which is acting as the glue but equally, they are almost completely committed to making a career change – and joining your company.

The basic technique is to open the discussion by asking what is causing their hesitation. At the same time, ask them to go over (and mutually discuss) the reasons behind them applying to your job vacancy in the first instance – what it was that appealed to them?

Remember that we are not talking about a counteroffer – although their cold feet may prompt them to have a discussion with their current employer. Perhaps not surprisingly, cold feet and counteroffers can overlap (both happen at the same time[41]).

This should be a relatively straightforward matter of uncovering the reasons for hesitating, and then going over how your offer addresses those points for them. If it comes down to leaving friendly colleagues behind (or loyalty to their current employer), your pitch must be about the strong points of your job offer, combined with the assurance you are a stable, warm, and welcoming employer (let's hope that's true!).

---

41. *It's worth asking if they have spoken to their current employer and if so, what have they said (most importantly, have they begun a counteroffer?) If the answer is yes, refer to the next subsection (Countering the counteroffer).*

Be prepared to allow them some time and space after your meeting (if they need it), although I recommend setting an expectation of signing on within a three-to-four-day period. This allows time for you to have additional discussions with your candidate but importantly, it says your organization will ultimately move on with another candidate if it needs to[42]. Let's now move on to the counteroffer issue because it's a little more complicated.

Countering the counteroffer

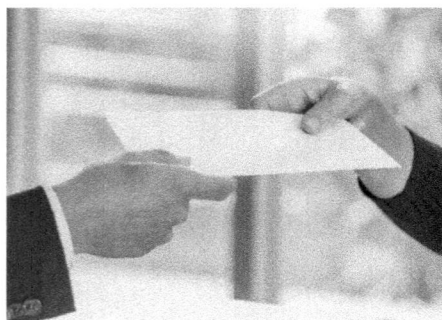

Sounds strange I know, but that's exactly what you will be doing. Once again, let' start with how a counteroffer usually unfolds from their current employer. Along the way, I'm going to highlight some "grab" points for you.

Most counteroffers begin when your offered candidate goes to talk to their current employer. This is your **first grab point**: Ask if they handed in their resignation during that initial discussion, or whether they simply went in to announce they had received an offer from another employer. If they handed in their resignation, you're on stronger ground (and more so if they did it in writing). If they simply went in to announce their alternate job offer, then it's often a signal that they are not fully disengaged from their current employer and are open to a counteroffer.

---

42. *Remember the advice in Chapter 9 to keep the other candidates on your shortlist warm, until your preferred candidate has signed on. Because until they have signed on, you still have a vacancy to fill.*

Let's assume for a moment they received a counteroffer. At first, this is usually extended verbally. Their current employer has probably canvassed a few talking points. Finding out what those talking points are, is your **second grab point**.

Counteroffer 1 - More money.

Any counteroffer substantially (or completely) based on an increase in their salary-wages, is the weakest of all counteroffers.

Technique 1A

Your response to a counteroffer of more money, should be to explain that their current employer has known that they (the candidate) has been worth more money for some time now, but they have been happy to get away with not paying it. In other words, they (the candidate) had to threaten to resign (or actually resign), in order to receive that additional money offer. In other words, their current employer has been taking advantage of them for some time. Pointing this out often opens the candidate's eyes to the insincerity of their current employer.

Past this, you do need to hope that the increased money offered is no more than what you are offering. Ideally, you should not enter a bidding war at this point. Your total offer (money, role and responsibilities, and the other benefits your job offer entails), were enough to see your candidate progress to The Offer Stage with you. Remind them of those other benefits. Don't make the discussion solely about money.

Technique 1B

Ask your candidate how the increased money offer would compare to their colleagues (peers). The reason? – very simply that if it places them above their colleagues (and their colleagues subsequently become aware of the amount of increase), then their relationship with their colleagues stands to change as a result. It's known as inequity theory – their colleagues are performing the same work but are now being paid less than your candidate. This causes further problems for the employer when it becomes known that "All you need to do to gain a pay increase here, is threaten to resign".

Counteroffer 2 – New or better responsibilities.

This will be harder to counter but only if the candidate is happy to keep working for their same employer, with the same products – services.

Technique 2A

Discuss with the candidate what those new responsibilities are. For example, are they substantially different and are they interesting enough? Compare them to what you are offering. They hopefully still fall short of your offer. Break down each duty and compare them equally. Are they creating an entirely new role for your candidate? Even if they are, break down your job responsibilities with the new, proposed ones of the counteroffer.

Technique 2B

Talk of new responsibilities and/or a new job with their existing employer is just that for the moment – talk. Ask your candidate when and if, their current employer will formalize their counteroffer. No one should be surprised that somewhere between trying to talk the candidate into staying and actually committing to paper, the current employer has overestimated their ability to change Job Descriptions. And why would that be? – simply because the bigger the proposed changes, the more likely they are to impact on other staff (including your candidate's colleagues) and their organization at large (how do they cover for the (presumably) old responsibilities they are saying the candidate can leave behind. **Third grab point** – request the candidate come back to you within a few days confirming (and hopefully showing you) the new responsibilities (counteroffer) on paper.

The big message

If they accept a counteroffer, it's very likely they will regret it.

Time to roll out the "big message" to your candidate if they are still undecided on whether to stay, or whether to join your company.

It's a reality that 70% of candidates who accept a counteroffer to remain with their existing employer, go on to *leave* that employer within the following 12 months.

Why would that be? Well, there are two main reasons:

The first is that (as mentioned above), their relationship with one or more of their colleagues' changes if they accept the counteroffer (which will almost always involve more money). Their relationship with their direct manager may also change - if the manager feels they were coerced into paying the candidate more money, under threat of the candidate leaving.

Secondly, and more crucially, because the underlying reasons for them wanting to leave their current place of employment, are *unlikely* to change.

While not mentioned up to this point, some candidates want to leave because they disagree with the direction their current employer is heading in. In addition, many want out because they have an unsatisfactory relationship with their direct manager (and it could be for a very sound reason). Or, as mentioned above, the products – services of their existing employer are staid (and yours are more interesting) etc.

You get the picture. The big-ticket reasons for looking elsewhere are exactly that (BIG).

Large, fundamental changes to organizations don't happen quickly, and your candidate is being (at least partly) sold on the prospect that they will. Open their eyes for them. It's a powerful technique. Use it.

All going to plan, you will have now successfully counselled your candidate through the counteroffer situation. If you've followed the relevant techniques outlined here and the candidate decides to stay with their existing employer, well, it was likely always going to be the case. Your candidate was never sufficiently committed to moving on and joining your company.

Although it is undoubtedly difficult to accept this outcome, you have in fact been spared from issues arising down the track with this candidate.

Of course, if they just needed to be reminded of the benefits of joining your company and you achieved that, then well done. You've landed that fish.

As you prepare your employment contract.

The one point I do want to emphasize as you extend your employment contract to the successful candidate, is to include a clause[43] as follows:

Any and all cited qualifications indicated either verbally or in written form – e.g.: resumé, website bio etc., are accurate, and all referees forwarded by you are genuine. Subsequent identification of false or misleading information will result in termination of your employment, and the company retains the right to take legal action against the employee for fraud or misrepresentation (as applicable).

---

43. *You need to first check this is permitted within the relevant employment laws of your country.*

Onboarding your new employee

Onboarding is a process of covering the workplace and employment laws in your country, combined with inducting the candidate to the specific requirements of your company, and the industry sector you operate in.

For Hiring's Secret Sauce, our value is in delivering a few tips / techniques for helping to "bed down" your new employee.

It's covered in our appendices.

Appendix 2 is known as "The Glue Section". It contains several reasons why the glue "holds", and your preferred candidate goes on to become a productive and valued employee. It is matched against a longer list of reasons why the glue "doesn't hold". The glue list is a "summing up" of experiences in this area and is, I hope, just a little bit of extra value in this book. It has a retention rather than onboarding focus.

For now, there's a simple way of looking at onboarding. Consider this episode from our "tales from the vault" series:

TALES FROM THE V🔒ULT

Well, not really…

Justin, a man who led a "colorful life" has just passed away from old age. He made it to 94. "Not bad" he thought to himself.

Next minute, Justin finds himself not at the pearly gates in front of St Peter, but in the fabled purgatory: that in-between place where one's ultimate fate is yet to be decided.

The man behind the desk recounts the bank robbery Justin took part in as a younger man. It went terribly wrong, and an innocent person was killed.

To decide his fate, Justin would spend one week in heaven, and one week in hell. He would then get to choose where he wanted to spend the remainder of eternity.

"A fair deal" he thought to himself. The express elevator took him to hell first.

As the elevator doors opened, he was greeted by the Devil, resplendent in an Armani suit, and a welcoming smile. He held out a glass of Justin's favourite Whisky. Behind him, a wild jazz band was playing (Justin's favourite music). In the distance he saw what looked like a fun park, some exotic female dancers, and if he wasn't mistaken, he could also see his best friends who now came running towards him - hugs and handshakes all around.

His friends told him that it's a continuous wild party with endless alcohol, great music, wonderful female company, and perfect California weather. You go to bed when you want, and get up when you want. No rules, no discipline. The ultimate free-wheeling lifestyle.

After one week of solid partying, Justin was returned to the elevator and whisked up to heaven.

The elevator now opened to a scene of white fluffy clouds, serene music, and angels playing harps. St Peter welcomes him and outlines how his time will be arranged.

"You will wake at 4.30am each morning, bring in the stars and the moon, and place the sun out for the day. You then have harp practice until 11am, followed by 7 hours of prayer and reflection. At 6pm you bring in the sun, and place the stars and moon back out again for the night. This will be your routine for the remainder of time".

Peter settles in and after one week is placed back in the elevator and returned to purgatory. The man behind the desk asks him: So, where's it to be?

"Easy" came the answer from Justin. Back downstairs. Back to my friends!

Instantaneously, Justin is transported back down below.

As the elevator doors open, a searing heat blasts Justin's face and body. The Devil (all red faced with horns and pitchfork) reaches into the elevator, grabs Justin by the throat and drags him out. There's no jazz music, no exotic dancers and his bedraggled friends are on a chain gang, being whipped by a demon. Large tumbleweeds roll across the barren and scorched landscape.

"But, where's the jazz music, exotic dancers, free alcohol, and partying? And what happened to my friends?".

"Easy" came the reply from the Devil. "Last week we were hiring. Today you're staff".

Sure, it's an old recruiter's joke – but it serves a purpose.

I would tell it to employers as a light-hearted way of explaining that if the reality of the job role (and just as importantly, the company's culture, financial health, products/services, and prospects for the future) weren't as they were claimed to be during the hiring process, then it is the number 1 reason why the glue doesn't hold.

Appendices

Appendix 1 –
Cooking the (Secret) Sauce

There's an extra little something you get when you put it all together. That something is another part of the method, although it's not a regular ingredient. Unlike a regular ingredient, it's not something you do, rather it's something that happens because you've used all the ingredients. A way to think of it, is that it's the final flavor you get when you cook the sauce. Up until then, all the individual ingredients were great, but put them all together and wow!

After several years of using the Secret Sauce, I realized there was an extra benefit I was receiving. It was something that came to life all on its own and played a significant part in getting the right result during my hiring exercises.

Back in Chapter 1 I used the term "right result" as a way of explaining that the Secret Sauce will just as often save you from hiring the wrong candidate, as it will confirm that you have found the right candidate.

A key reason why the Secret Sauce delivers, is because it places your preferred candidate in an environment which overcomes any attempt to adopt a different persona, or portray themselves as something (or someone) they're not.

Time + Different Perspectives

Some people in their normal lives can (if they so desire), put across a little white lie or two, or perhaps act differently to how they really are. Their motives may be unknown and are hopefully minor – possibly something that the listener doesn't care much about and is unlikely to scrutinize (think: two people meeting in a social setting for the first time). In other words, such people get accepted on face value. However, if they make a habit of it, eventually the listener begins to have some doubts and may slowly form a different opinion about their new friend.

Getting to the doubting stage between acquaintances usually requires an amount of time. Certainly, more time than the usual hiring exercise takes.

However, if a candidate chooses to do this during a hiring exercise, it's usually in the hope of a substantial gain (think: claiming a qualification that isn't true, or an inflated workplace achievement). For a bit of reference, look back to The Dirty Dozen lies found in Chapter 7 and The Interview Masterclass series in Chapter 10.

Telling a lie in a resumé, or exaggerating an achievement in an interview, carries a risk. The risk is that the candidate gets found out and is subsequently disqualified.

But, looking at this in terms of lies and exaggerations isn't what we're talking about here. Those actions are overt, and easy enough to spot using the methods outlined in this book.

In a reasonable number of cases though, candidates are intent on presenting themselves as different or better than they actually are. This is where the term "adopting a different persona" comes into play.

Certain candidates who are aware of their weaknesses (or understand the effect their personality has on others), will attempt to mask or alter those aspects of their personality throughout the hiring exercise.

Think of it as holding your breath (but for a lot longer). It's killing you, and you really need to exhale.

As an example, imagine for a moment a person who has a bad temper, evident only during times of workplace pressure or stress. The hiring environment is different to almost anything else the average person encounters during their life. As you follow the Secret Sauce steps, your preferred candidate(s), are being placed under a degree of pressure.

Using the above example, I will often encounter raised voices, or a nervousness (even a bluntness), under direct questioning.

In addition, I will hear certain muted comments from referees, or the employer (my client – you in this example), will feed back that something was a little strange during their interview.

And here we get to the crux of the *something extra* in the sauce.

As an employer, you need to obtain different perspectives on your preferred candidate(s). Without a recruiter involved to give you that different perspective, you need to involve at least one other person in your company. While a panel interview (refer Chapter 11) is one technique to use, I recommend you share out the reference checking with a colleague. Taking your preferred candidate(s) for a tour of your company (where they are introduced to several other staff members) is also an effective technique.

Once you have organized your different perspectives, the other technique working for you is time. That is to say, the natural time your hiring exercise will take. Typically, from first contact (phone screening or resumé review), through to offering the job, it's generally a two-to-four-week time period.

Cracks in a candidate's story - or their ability to maintain a different persona, are almost always overcome by the individual steps (ingredients) of the Secret Sauce, plus time, plus different perspectives.

Here's how the "something extra" in the Secret Sauce plays out:

1. Multiple points of contact (yourself and other staff).
2. Multiple types of contact (resumé review, phone screening, interview, second interview, psychometric assessment, reference checks), and
3. Across time.

The ability of a candidate to maintain a false persona under all these conditions and steps, is extremely difficult and, in my experience, rare.

This has worked so effectively for me over the last twenty years that, you guessed it – we've got our fourteenth and final ingredient of The Secret Sauce. It's not one of the catchiest ingredient titles I've got, so I thought I'd write it up as a formula...

> **HIRING'S SECRET SAUCE**
>
> **Multiple points of contact + multiple types of contacts + time**

Appendix 2 – "The Glue"

When I first began working in a large agency, I was told it would take between eighteen months and two years to become an accomplished recruiter. That was mostly true, though in retrospect, I realized that by the two-year mark, I had only seen and experienced about 90% of everything I would experience. It then took approximately five more years to experience the remaining 10%. That's seven years of full-time recruitment work. There were some early failures which I began to term "The glue". If I got the hire "right", the glue tended to hold, and it was a long-term fruitful arrangement for both candidate and employer. But, If I got it wrong, the glue was weak and didn't hold. It became apparent that there were just a handful of reasons which made the glue hold, but many, many, more "issues" that made the glue weak and less likely to hold.

Written up as an appendix, I hope it provides a little extra value to this book.

Reasons why the glue holds

1. The salary is as promised and (hopefully) represents a small increase.

2. The reality of the job is as outlined in the Job Description and the advert.
3. The "picture" of the company – its products, services, market position, prospects for the future etc., are as outlined during the hiring process (e.g.: there was no "overselling").
4. The company culture is good.
5. The role brings new or varied duties and responsibilities, which increases job satisfaction.
6. They experience a good working relationship with their (new) direct manager and colleagues.

Reasons why the glue doesn't hold

1. The company, its products-services, prospects for the future, etc. are not as they were indicated through the hiring process.
2. As above, (but in some other way), you oversold the role and/or your company.
3. A demanding manager with unrealistic performance expectations.
4. The salary is the same as their previous employment (the glue is not strong).
5. The salary is not as promised (perhaps a range was indicated, and the employment contract was written at the lower end of that range?).
6. The candidate voluntarily accepts a lower salary-wage. This typically becomes an issue within a few months when major expenses arise. Some candidates join in the belief that their wages will soon increase.
7. There are no prospects for advancement.
8. There is no personal development on offer – no opportunity to grow their skills.

9. There are no prospects to earn more through greater productivity or output.

10. The "culture" of the company is uninspiring.

11. A conflict occurs with existing staff, or the new employee does not suit (or fit in) with your company culture.

12. The candidate (new employee) feels that your company experiences occasional cashflow problems, or in some other way, is not financially secure.

13. The candidate was incorrectly matched to your company (see section below on A to D ratings).

14. Downshifting was imminent (see below).

15. The personal drivers of the candidate were changing (see below).

16. For sales positions, not being up-front about the realistic chances of achieving bonuses, which the candidate may have factored into their normal earnings.

17. For sales positions, not being up-front about the true level of self-generated leads or cold calling required to either achieve bonuses, or even to remain employed.

18. For entry level roles, a near equivalent job is identified with reduced commute times and/or, better amenities and local services.

Others. I'm sorry to say I've probably forgotten a few, but these 18 certainly cover the major reasons.

Matching companies to candidates

Matching is something that the best recruiters instinctively do during the hiring process, and it's a significant factor when it comes to the glue. A simple A to D rating system for both employer and candidate provides an easy method to ensure you are getting it right from the very first contact (resumé review and phone screen). Within these A to D categories there can exist a wide variation on both sides, so remain a little flexible in your ratings. A simple philosophy to embrace is "know your candidate's abilities and aspirations" and "be honest about who and what your company is – and what it offers". If for example you are a C-level company, then endeavoring to attract B, let alone A rated candidates, will either be unsuccessful from the outset, or see the glue fail within a short time of commencement.

A to D level companies (employers)[44]

A. A-level companies are blue-chip companies which are usually listed on the stock exchange. Think: The Global Top 500 – i.e.: Microsoft, Amazon, Meta, Apple etc.

B. B-level companies are generally privately owned. B level companies have some brand awareness (if not among the public,) then certainly within their industry sector. Employee numbers tend to be 100 + and they may operate in many different states or countries.

C. C-level are small to medium companies (typically 20 – 100 staff). The level of business sophistication tends to be lower with C level companies. While it can vary significantly, on average these companies may not have well-defined business policies and procedures. Their level of business sophistication may be low to medium. They can still be innovative and industry leaders, or they can be more reactionary in response to market conditions.

D. D-level. These are small companies (1 – 20 employees). They are usually unsophisticated and have less of a track record[45]. Their longevity may be unknown. Prospects for advancement are often low.

A to D Candidates (Non industry specific/generic)[46]

A. A-rated candidates are professional and degree qualified (not necessarily management – e.g.: might be at operational level such

---

44. *Please note that these A to D company ratings have no equivalence to academic scoring (where A is excellent, and D is almost a fail). It is merely a reducing scale of size, market power, capability etc.*

45. *Conversely, D companies can comprise start-ups which have a great future in front of them. Know your story is the mantra here.*

as an engineer, accountant, technical specialist etc.) with a proven track record of success. They are career builders (looking to maintain or improve their current level of remuneration, and/or seeking career advancement). Typically, the resumé's of A-rated candidates contain A-rated employers, and they continue to seek out employment in publicly listed or large private companies. Their referees are solid.

B. Similar to A-rated candidates but typically found working for B level companies. They add value to their employers and can cite verifiable achievements. B-rated candidates are professional, and career minded. They may or may not be degree qualified, and do not necessarily seek out employment in large, publicly listed companies. Their referees are also solid.

C. C-rated candidates are not usually degree qualified but can be. They are normally qualified to diploma or certificate level. These candidates do worthwhile things for their employers and are viewed as scoring mid-to-upper range for productivity and effectiveness. In comparison to their A and B rated counterparts, they are less inclined to be career builders and are often focused on maintaining their current employment and conditions. Their referees are good rather than excellent.

D. Many D-rated candidates are unqualified except where minor qualifications or licenses are required to perform their chosen work. D-rated candidates still deliver results, but are prepared to live with lower business sophistication. They are generally content to work for D-level companies. Referees for D-rated candidates may be variable in their quality and reliability.

In summary, an employer who attempts to convince an A or B rated candidate to join a C or D level company, will either be unsuccessful up-front, or find the glue doesn't hold within a short period of time.

---

46. *Once again, an A to D rating for candidates relates purely to their level of qualifications, demonstrable skills, abilities and career aspirations. It is not in any way a personal assessment or valuation.*

Danger on the downshift...

This one deserved its own mini section for the sheer frustration it can cause. Downshifting is a term that originates in driving automobiles. When you wanted to slow down, you shifted the gears downwards from 6th to 5th to 4th etc. Your speed then went down as a result. Candidates who are downshifters want a reduction in pace (or intensity) with respect to their working lives.

When you encounter this in a candidate (and they typically won't say it outright), well, it's usually not a good thing. You're very likely going to meet some of these candidates (whom you might rate highly).

Your interview proforma will probably look good – but you can certainly identify downshifters during your first interview and most definitely, by your second interview or reference checking.

Often, the desire to downshift is found in Managers. Many have worked for larger companies (let's assume an example of an A or B rated candidate). Hypothetically, your company might be a C level company. In essence, you recognize they can bring advanced skills to your business. The candidate simply doesn't want to work as long or as hard as they have been, and both sides see a potential match. The candidate may not make it clear that they are looking to reduce their excessive daily hours, so it's up to you to uncover their work preferences for the future.

The punchline is that they will almost always want to retain their present level of remuneration – which typically will be a stretch for your company.

I've always counselled employers against hiring downshifters or at the very least, to have very frank discussions about performance expectations. If you employ them, you may find it's just the tip of the iceberg as they have effectively made the switch from work-life balance to life-work balance (their focus has inverted). An example is discussed in Chapter 9 with a candidate named John who wanted to spend more time on his recently acquired rural property.

Downshifters are out there, but fortunately the Secret Sauce method provides everything you need to identify them. Keep a look out…

Old colleagues and peers

Ah yes, the good old days. They might have moved on. Have you?

A final word here is on the potential challenges that come with candidates that you either worked with years earlier, or were a well-regarded peer at another company.

This challenge broaches the concepts of The Halo Effect and Gut Instinct (themes covered in Chapter 9).

The first issue - especially with an old colleague, is to assume they are the same person you worked with all those years ago. There's a distinct possibility that changes in their career goals, their financial position, personal life, education level, etc. has changed their focus. They know it, but your perception of them is still rooted back in those old days.

Your best approach? – step back, if possible, from the hiring process in favor of a colleague. And whichever way you go, advise the candidate they will be subjected to all the hiring steps. It's the right thing to do for your company – and for the candidate.

This also holds true for a previous contact who may have worked at a certain level in the past, but is now intent on "moving up".

For reference, look back to Chapter 9 and the case of an analyst who, after investing his own money successfully, now feels less inclined to work solid ten-hour days – or the IT technician that felt it was now time to "move up" to Project Management rather than remain "on the tools".

Sticky fingers?

Making it stick is really what good hiring is all about. You need that employer-employee bond to be strong, and some of the tip's contained here in Appendix 2 should help you achieve that.

Keep a look out for these "glue clues" and use the various techniques and insights as and when they become appropriate.

Best of luck.

Appendix 3 – Performance Management

I've always had a bit of an issue with performance management…

In essence, I always wondered why it was needed - assuming you hired correctly in the first place. And that's still how I feel today. Of course, there are legitimate times where performance management (P.M) is required. Whenever I encounter organizations that are "performance managing" an employee, I either find a mismatch to the J.D (when they initially hired the individual) or legitimately, that output is not what it once was. If it's the latter, then the need to P.M should (generally) only be required after a significant period of time, and in my experience, is usually not successful long-term.

Performance management shouldn't be confused with career coaching or development, which are positive actions to build or improve an employee's skill set.

As you moved through this book, you would have found a major theme of finding motivated and driven candidates with verifiable work histories. Where that is the case, you can expect to find responsible, "self-winding"[47] individuals, who would be taking matters into their own hands – i.e.: by either recognizing the need to lift their output, or by resigning and moving on.

Admittedly, I'm talking mainly about white-collar employees here.

Performance management is only ever a temporary activity, and it can't be part of your long-term business strategy. That's because it's impractical and unprofitable for management to continuously monitor and drive acceptable output (for a specific employee). This is where the concept of self-winding comes into play.

Hiring's Secret Sauce is about identifying candidates who are self-motivated and can therefore be left to deliver average or above-average output on a continuous basis.

---

47. *Much like an old-fashioned watch, these employees are self-winding in terms of their motivation. They don't need to be coaxed into action, nor do they require constant oversight just to achieve acceptable levels of performance.*

Certainly, I've encountered employees who benefitted from some short-term P.M (and it helped them mostly regain their former levels of output) however, I have to say that in almost every case, it wasn't sustainable long-term – i.e.: the employee ultimately lapsed again.

At the very least then, performance management is something that should only happen very infrequently.

Plan to avoid it altogether by hiring capable, self-winding employees.

Appendix 4 – Burgers, Bank Managers, and Business Plans. *(Is A.I a bit over-egged?)*

The following content was originally part of Chapter 4, but during the editing process, I found that it didn't quite fit the general narrative, so it has been placed here instead. This content is designed to give those who may want to understand a little more about A.I programs, a clearer picture of what these programs could reasonably expect to do for someone in business. Now, depending on when you're reading this, A.I (as an emerging technology) could be quite different to the example provided on the next page.

A.I (Artificial Intelligence **or All Invasive?**).

There could be a few factors to consider with the emergence of A.I but for mine, it's the observation that A.I has imprinted itself on the minds of so many consumers (so many of us) – because we're all consumers.

We are daily, bombarded by products and services which have the acronym "A.I" either placed in front of them, or embedded somewhere within their name. If you're like me, you might struggle to understand what's especially "intelligent" about many of these products and services. In some cases (e.g.: within the hiring space) I recognize some of these "new" A.I products as the same tools I had at my disposal when I first went to work in a large agency (i.e.: a long time ago). It's because of this large time gap that I began to wonder what these companies were actually selling (because they certainly weren't offering anything substantially new). So, A.I has become very pervasive, but the question remains, just how intelligent is it? To find out, let's now jump into the content lifted from Chapter 4.

This was an exercise conducted with the main A.I programs to see how they could help an imaginary start-up venture. Specifically, the start-up was a new café that would specialize in burgers. It was an interesting exercise, and it went like this:

How do you like your burger – real meat or plant based? (I asked A.I)

For the most part, A.I programs take all the data/knowledge in their possession and, when asked a specific question, extrapolate that data (move it forward) to a conclusion of sorts. Think of it this way: If an A.I program is able to access the Internet in deeper and more thorough ways than you can via your search engine (and it certainly can), then it might know that the amount of non-meat hamburgers being consumed across the world is growing at a faster rate than the consumption of beef burgers. It might also then compile data on how many vegetarians there are in the world. It may even know the rate of growth of vegetarians. Moving along further, it might be able to find out how many new non-meat products were introduced across the world in each of the last three years[48].

Because you are thinking of opening a new burger café in your part of the world, you might ask the A.I program what types of burgers are most likely to sell. From its answers, you could set your menu, establish your suppliers and start your business with (perhaps) more confidence. Its answers might inform you that your new burger cafe should offer five different types of non-meat burger, and only two beef burgers.

You might have begun all of this by asking the program: "I'm thinking of opening up a hamburger café in Portland, Oregon, USA. What types of burgers should I sell to give me the best chance of success?".

What we're talking about here is market research and business information.

Now obviously, the A.I program isn't going to lease the café for

---

48. *I'm being far too generous. The A.I program could not answer a single question relating to our burger example.*

you, let alone cook the burgers and serve them, but there's no doubt you got some benefit from it.

And if you do open that café, in time your A.I program might be able to place orders on your suppliers in the timeliest fashion – or help you get the best price for your ingredients.

I know what you're thinking right now... you're picturing a time where the ingredients arrive at the rear door of the café, and the burgers are cooked and assembled by a series of machines. Finally, a robot resembling Rosie from the old cartoon series "The Jetsons", delivers it to the customers at their table. Possible?- yes. In fact, it can be done now by the cutting-edge of robotics and A.I, but it's going to be some years yet before it's affordable or viable for a café. And there's the other factor, – will customers really line up for robots cooking and serving them a meal, or will they head to your competitor – you know, the one with the staff who have a welcoming smile and a funny story to share?

When the rubber hits the road...

This is a saying from the car racing industry. It's a euphemism for "when things get real". If you are going to use A.I to construct your

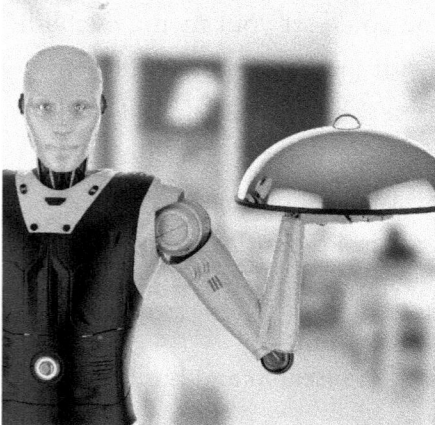

I'll take mine with a little more soul please.

business plan for that new burger café, there will come a point where you need to front up to a bank to secure a loan for that café. If you hand over an A.I written business plan to your bank manager, do you think they will accept it and extend you a loan on that basis?

If you hide this fact from them (and the A.I plan makes good sense), then the answer might be yes. But if you admit up-front that it isn't your own work, then perhaps not.

But, it might not be wise to take a guess on this, so I contacted a bank manager to ask this exact question. The short answer is that you will have to provide financial projections. If the bank deems those projections to be reasonable (and you can provide collateral – quite possibly the home you own) then sure, – because once you sign that loan document, the bank has all the security they need.

This is a round-about way of saying that if you want to rely on an A.I generated business plan, then you would want to be very confident because they (the bank), have got all the collateral they need from you.

The point of this exercise is to demonstrate a task that A.I might reasonably be expected to perform[49], to the benefit of a start-up business. The answer is that A.I can extract, compile and potentially extrapolate known information from the internet, but dealing with people is an entirely different prospect.

So, the question is, are you feeling lucky, p#@k? …with apologies to Clint Eastwood.

---

49. *Once again, the A.I program couldn't perform any of the burger tasks indicated here. A.I is just not there yet.*

Appendix 5 – List the Secret Sauce ingredients here

Ingredient 1:	
Ingredient 2:	
Ingredient 3:	
Ingredient 4:	
Ingredient 5:	
Ingredient 6:	
Ingredient 7:	
Ingredient 8:	
Ingredient 9:	
Ingredient 10:	
Ingredient 11:	
Ingredient 12:	
Ingredient 13:	
Ingredient 14:	

End Notes

Note 1. Tales From the Vault series. Real or not? Yes, it all happened as outlined*. There were more, but they didn't support the various ingredients especially well, and to be honest, some were more shock value than lesson-learning. A few involved employers, not just candidates. It is surprising what some people will say and do when there is a potential job in the offing, and just as surprising how some employers will behave, just because they enjoy a power advantage. It's worth mentioning again that only good employers attract good candidates.

Note 2. Is there more information I have, more that I could tell you? The answer is yes, there is, but the extra content had to give way to the method this book teaches.

A lot of the additional information is very nuanced and is mostly about subtle techniques or additional candidate insights. While that might have interested some of you, it equally stood to bog down many readers with an excess of detail – and I didn't want that.

I also promised no stats, no graphs, and no big data etc., and at least some of the extra material would have required graphs. This book is supposed to be a relatively easy read. If the demand is there, there might be a follow-up – perhaps a true pocket size companion with several advanced techniques to really elevate your hiring skills.

Until then, I'll leave you with one of my well-used sayings (to employers) when they were undecided about whether to proceed with a certain candidate or not: "A maybe is a no".

* *Refer to the References section for more detail.*

References (Content)

There aren't any.

I was dismayed recently when I purchased a book from a newly minted entrepreneur. I skimmed the chapter titles in the bookstore and was particularly taken with the cover artwork. The chapter layouts and copywriting also looked good, so I purchased it with the plan of a weekend read.

As I got underway, I quickly discerned that the book contained many (in fact, very many) concepts and ideas I had heard before. I quickly jumped to the reference page(s) at the end of the book. I was disappointed (but not surprised) at the sheer volume of referenced works. My disappointment was due to the audacity of this fellow charging what he was charging for the book (and trust me, he doesn't need the extra money), with nary a shred of new thinking. Good form alone would dictate you sell a book in the belief you're imparting some new knowledge – not just a rehash of everything that's been said before.

Now, while I'm not claiming that what I have to say is all new, I've at least done my research and have not been able to identify another book of this style - nor substantially with this content[50]. What I am standing on is over twenty years of lived experience as a recruiter – and as a developer of tools for the purpose of hiring and variously, to support candidates in their search for employment.

As a final word here on references, you will notice that percentages are occasionally quoted throughout the book. These percentages were derived from my own twenty-plus years of hiring experience.

---

50. *Of course, if I'm wrong and you do have something to say on this, then I expect I'll hear from your lawyers (but I hope not).*

References (People)

Characters and Tales From The Vault (Series)

The recollections contained in this book as they relate to events, are mine alone, and are recalled to the best of my ability using a combination of personal interactions, interview and reference check notes, psychometric assessment reports, and other source material and processes used by me.

The names of individuals and employers cited throughout this book have been altered, and the employers genericized to guard the privacy of the actual individuals and companies involved. Minutia within the events have been further altered – e.g.: specific occupations, locations, other individuals present, etc.

Not another acknowledgement page

I'm not sure about you, but I just don't get much from the average acknowledgement page. We tend to hear about the author's inspiration – along with the support they received from the love of their life and the companionship of their ever-faithful labradoodle "Bo Bo" who stuck it out for months while they hammered away on the keys.

Sure, that's all fine, but I thought it better just to give you a picture of what the author is actually like, by sharing some of the remarks and observations delivered to me in person (or overheard) from colleagues, clients, and friends over the years.

Here we go:

"Somewhat hard-nosed, but a friend nevertheless."

"Meticulous. Would rather be called a time-waster than deliver sub-standard work."

"Opinionated would be one word. In fact, probably the only word that's relevant."

"Seems to be resilient and adaptable."

"Very honest and trustworthy."

"Mostly a likeable guy. Mostly."

"Drinks more espresso coffee than anyone I've ever met."

"Never really sure what he's thinking. May be hiding something."

"Keeps coming back for more – even when he shouldn't."

And, my personal favorite: "The best recruiter I've ever known."

Not hard to see why I like that last remark so much.

Gary Costa is a 24 year veteran of the recruitment industry, where he continues to develop products for use by employers and job seekers. He began his recruiting career in Australia's largest and most prestigious agency (Morgan & Banks). Prior to recruitment he worked in high-tech manufacturing, operating across R&D, Product Development, Marketing and Distribution. He travelled extensively across Asia and Europe, evaluating major projects for viability, training distributors, and pitching to global clients.

He is a Fellow of The Institute of Managers and Leaders (Australia), and holds business qualifications from Monash University (Australia).

* Bragging rights conferred if you can guess the background.